SCRUPLES AND SAINTHOOD

Accepting and Overcoming Scrupulosity with the Help of the Saints

by Trent Beattie

*Heaven is filled with converted sinners of all kinds
and there is room for more.*

—Saint Joseph Cafasso

Imprimatur: † Most Rev. Alex J. Brunett
Archbishop of Seattle
August 17, 2010

Published by Loreto Publications 2011

ISBN: 9781930278-96-9

All Rights Reserved

Printed in Canada

Loreto Publications
P. O. Box 603
Fitzwilliam, NH 03447
www.loretopubs.org

Dedication

Free your mind from all that troubles you;
God will take care of things.
                                    – Saint Vincent de Paul

This book is dedicated to Saint Alphonsus Liguori (1696–1787), bishop, founder of two religious orders, the most published author in history* and fellow sufferer of scrupulosity, who was named a Doctor of the Church by Pope Pius IX in 1871, and patron of moralists and confessors by Pope Pius XII in 1950. The man who was tormented at times by anxiety, confusion, and doubt in regard to issues of conscience, is the same man whom Catholics are officially encouraged to call upon for help in those very same matters.

The great Italian saint knew well what agony the scrupulous can go through, saying, "Scrupulosity is one of the most bitter trials souls who love God can undergo, worse than ill-health, persecutions, and similar sufferings." He knew about the topic not simply from study, but from personal encounter. If anyone is looking for a saint to help him deal with scrupulosity, it is Saint Alphonsus Liguori. While many other saints have suffered from bouts of scruples and do have very helpful things to say on the matter, Saint Alphonsus seems uniquely qualified to offer just the right advice on the subject, emphasizing prayer, obedience, and resignation to God's will.

Saint Alphonsus, patron of moralists and confessors, pray for us, that we may place our trust not in ourselves, but in divine mercy and providence, that we may see that God wills our good infinitely better than we could ever do it ourselves, that He has spared nothing for our salvation, giving us His only-begotten Son. May we see in all things the holy will of God, especially in the decisions of His ministers. We ask this with our heavenly patron and model Saint Alphonsus as we ask all things, through Christ Our Lord, Amen. Mary, Mother of God, pray for us.

Let these souls so dear to God, and who are resolutely determined to belong entirely to Him, take comfort, although at the same time they see themselves deprived of every consolation. Their desolation is a sign of their being very acceptable to God, and that He has for them a place prepared in his heavenly Kingdom, which overflows with consolations as full as they are lasting. And let them hold for certain, that the more they are afflicted in this present life, so much the more they shall be consoled in eternity: 'According to the multitude of my sorrows in my heart, Thy comforts have given joy to my soul'. (Ps. 93:19).

–Saint Alphonsus Liguori

*The writings of Saint Alphonsus have been printed in more editions—well over 21,000—than those of any other author. For more on this, see page 623 of *33 Doctors of the Church* by Father Christopher Rengers, O.F.M., Cap. (TAN Books)

Table Of Contents

Introduction

We have all heard the saying, after someone has fretted over something for a long period of time, perhaps rearranging it over and over again, that it is 'good enough.' Not that it is fantastic, unparalleled, or completely perfect, but that it is 'good enough.'

There may be many times we would like to do something over or improve upon it, but the non-scrupulous seem more able to let go and move on when such an impulse confronts them. They are able to 'leave well enough alone' and focus their attention on other things. Scrupulous souls, on the other hand, have trouble leaving things as they are, and instead worry about whether or not they are 'good enough.'

This worry over the state of external things is directly related to worry over the state of one's own soul. While it is true that God calls us to perfection, He does not expect us to be flawless immediately. Christian perfection is the work (first and foremost of God) of a lifetime, and is completed when we reach Heaven.

Also, Christian perfection is decidedly different from 'perfectionism,' in which someone relies on himself in a futile attempt never to do anything wrong and to be better than everyone else, out of the motives of pride and vanity. Indeed, scrupulosity could be defined as spiritual vanity. Someone who is vain about material things constantly wonders, "How do I look, how do I look?" while someone who is vain about spiritual things constantly wonders, "How does my soul look? How does my soul look?"

Instead of wanting utterly comprehensive and flawless confessions, perfectly enunciated prayers, or even no hair out of place on our heads, God really wants our love. He wants us to love Him above all else, and to love our neighbor for the love of Him. When asked what the greatest commandment is, Our Lord declared "Thou shalt love the Lord thy God with thy whole heart and with thy whole soul and with thy whole mind. This is the greatest and the first commandment. And the second is like this: Thou shalt love thy neighbor as thyself" (Mt. 22:37-39).

A greater appreciation of the means of salvation the saints have used will enable the scrupulous soul to be more closely united with the Holy Trinity, through sanctifying grace. This grace is the love of God for souls, a love He enables us to return to Him through the theological virtue charity—the most necessary of all virtues—by which we love God above all else, and our neighbor as ourselves for the love of God. As Saint Anthony Mary Claret (1807-1870) states, "The most necessary virtue of all is love. Yes, I have said it once, and I will say it a thousand times . . ."

This little book is not meant to be a comprehensive manual with all the answers to all the questions that may come up in the fight against scrupulosity. Instead, it is a tool to help bring about sainthood, to which we are all called. Let us not deceive ourselves; our problems do not keep us from becoming saints; *our problems help us to become saints, if we so will.* The important thing is not the outward problem or challenge we face, but *how we face it*—that is, how we see it and in turn, respond to it. As Saint Alphonsus says, "Many things appear to us to be misfortunes, but if we understood the end for which God sends them, we would see that they are graces," adding, "Contradictions, sickness, scruples, spiritual aridity and all the inner and outward torments are the chisel with which God carves his statues for Heaven."

Chapter One:
Defining the Problem

The suffering that affects scrupulous souls comes from the fear
that what they are doing might be sinful.

—Saint Alphonsus Liguori

The word "scruple" comes from the Latin for "pebble". It takes a large rock for most people to stumble over, yet for the scrupulous, a pebble can be a stumbling block. A simple definition of a scruple is a groundless fear of having sinned, when in fact no sin was committed. Scrupulous souls can spend much time obsessing over trivial matters, taking time from things that actually do matter.

Scrupulous souls live in a state of fear, unsure of where they stand in relation to God and others. Imagined, sometimes contradictory, obligations occupy their minds and make clear thinking very difficult. The result can be odd behavior, trying to do two different things at the same time, repeating an action many times to make sure it 'takes', or randomly changing one's mind and course of action.

Saint Alphonsus Liguori, who himself suffered from scrupulosity at certain times, tells us some signs of a scrupulous conscience: holding out against advice, obstinacy of judgment, frequent changes of mind, being concerned about irrelevant ideas, and fear of sin in everything. Additionally, scrupulous souls often have misconceptions about Church teaching (erring on the more rigorous side) and, in an attempt to be holy, rely on their own strength rather than the grace of God. It is easy to see, with all these characteristics, that another problem of the scrupulous can be thinking that salvation is impossible or nearly so.

The cause of scrupulosity can be physical, mental, emotional, or spiritual; or a mixture of two or more of these aspects. At times, one or more of these aspects can be a contributing factor to the problem, but not necessarily the cause. Someone in ill health may be prone to scruples, as may someone suffering under mental strain from overwork, or, interestingly enough, someone who is not occupied with enough work, or someone who is emotionally insecure, or someone with sincere misconceptions about spiritual matters.

Many people have at one time or another been the victim of scrupulous thoughts, but not all these people could be properly classified as scrupulous in general. Who has not been obstinate, or changed his mind about something more than once, or been concerned about irrelevant ideas? The difference between a scrupulous soul and one who has been bothered by a particular scruple is the frequency and intensity of the problem.

If there are intense fears about possible sin that regularly affect your peace of mind, then you are dealing with scrupulosity.

Note well that the problem does not consist of fears about *certain sin*—a fear which everyone should have, to some extent. This is the key to scrupulosity: it is not the fear of *certain sin,* but intense, continuous fear of *the possibility of sin.* If you are troubled about *certain sin,* what is needed is acceptance that you committed it, knowledge that God's mercy is infinitely more powerful than your sin (and all the sins of the world combined), and finding a good priest to whom you can confess the sin in the sacrament of Reconciliation. If this course of action frightens you, pray for the grace to do it, and God will give it to you. Ask and you shall receive. Saint Alphonsus states confidently,

> Prayer obtains every grace that is asked for; it vanquishes all the strength of the tempter and it changes men from blind into seeing, from weak into strong, from sinners into saints. Let him who wants light ask it of God, and it shall be given . . . God gives to all the grace of prayer, in order that thereby they may obtain every help, and even more than they need, for keeping the divine law . . .

If, on the other hand, you are regularly troubled about *possible sins,* the remedy is a little different, which is precisely what this book is for. Continuing on this theme, let us look a little more closely at the concerns of the scrupulous.

Scrupulous souls tend to have irrelevant ideas about certain situations. This is a product of fear, which is the generator of such ideas. Fear, and more specifically, fear of sin, is the main characteristic of the scrupulous, who tend to fear the occurrence of sin in every situation. Sometimes the ideas generated by fear can be so irrelevant that they are in fact seen as amusing, even by the scrupulous soul himself, when he has attained a more peaceful state of mind.

For example, say a man on his way into church is thinking about how one's soul should be clean in order to receive Holy Communion. He starts to wonder about the state of his own soul, fretting about this and that action in his past possibly being sinful, but does not come to any definite conclusions in the matter. After waving to some friends in the parking lot, the man steps up onto the sidewalk, and inadvertently crushes a spider with his shoe.

The man then wonders if maybe he should not receive Holy Communion—after all, he just killed something. What is more, one's soul should be clean in order to receive Holy Communion, and the sole of his foot is not clean. This might be a sign of something greater—his spiritual *soul* may not be clean either. The man worries and worries about this clean sole/soul dilemma. For the scrupulous person unaware of the concept of doubt (which is covered in Chapter Five), such a trivial thing may actually become an occasion of losing peace of mind, and in turn, of not receiving Holy Communion.

A scrupulous soul familiar with the concept of doubt will be able to laugh at the whole thing, seeing how silly it is. There is no commandment to keep our shoes clean, and the Church does *not* teach that the cleanness of our shoes is analogous to the cleanness of our souls. What would you think of a person who came up to you and said, "Look at how clean my shoes are—I am going to Heaven for sure!" When our doubts are put in the right perspective, we see how small they are, and we can actually laugh at them, taking them as lightly as we would take a dead spider on the sidewalk.

In addition to the signs of a scrupulous conscience, Saint Alphonsus also tells us some remedies, namely: cultivating humility; avoiding rigorous or harsh books and scrupulous people; avoiding idleness, where meaningless fears influence us; not spending a lot of time on examination of conscience, *especially on those things that are the occasion of most trouble,* and vehemently cultivating trust in God, which is manifested in obedience to a spiritual director. These topics will be addressed more fully in later chapters.

It should be noted here, however, that in addition to avoiding rigorous books and the company of other scrupulous people, we should also read good books and be in the company of devout, stable, solid Catholics. We cannot solve our problems on our own, so we should look to others within the Church for support.

Saint Paul tells us in 1 Corinthians 12:14–27:

> For as the body is one and hath many members; and all the members of the body, whereas they are many, yet are one body: so also *is* Christ. For in one Spirit were we all baptized into one body, whether Jews or Gentiles, whether bond or free: and in one Spirit we have all been made to drink. For the body also is not one member, but many. If the foot should say: Because I am not the hand, I am not of the body: Is it therefore not of the body? And if the ear should say: Because I am not the eye, I am not of the body: Is it therefore not of the body? If the whole body were the eye, where would be the hearing? If the whole were hearing, where would be the smelling? But now God hath set the members, everyone set the members, every one of them, in the body as it hath pleased him. And if they all were one member, where would be the body? But now *there are* many members indeed, yet one body. And the eye cannot say to the hand: I need not thy help. Nor again the head to the feet: I have no need of you. . .. And if one member suffer anything, all the members suffer with it: or if

> one member glory, all the members rejoice with
> it. Now you are the body of Christ and members
> of member.

This is an amazing description of the followers of Christ by Saint Paul. He does not say that we are a community, or even a family, but *a body*—the body of Christ. We are so closely connected with other Christians as to form one body, with Christ as our head. This is a tremendously important reality for the scrupulous to realize.

In order to get a better perspective on the situation and help the healing process, we should connect, or reconnect, with other members of the body of Christ. This can be done first and foremost by participating in the sacraments, which unite us more fully to Christ, and therefore to each other. The sacraments were entrusted to the Church by Our Lord not for veneration from afar, but for our own reverent use. Also of help are prayer groups, Bible or catechism studies, and participating in other parish activities.

When we interact with others, we can see ourselves more clearly. Everyone has a cross (or several) to bear, which becomes much more visible to us as we get closer to others. When we are far removed from others, unreasonable and inaccurate ideas about them can get into our heads. We can get the conception of others not having any problems, which only encourages us to feel worse about our own problems. We can feel as if it is somehow unusual to have anything go wrong, when in fact this happens every day for every one on earth. No one has a 'perfect day', in the sense that everything he set out to accomplish was done in exactly the manner he had planned. We all have difficulties to deal with, and this becomes much more clear when we interact with others.

OTHERS OUTSIDE THE BODY OF CHRIST

It is true that we can be influenced by others in a negative way, so we should generally avoid the company of those who lead immoral lives. We should not go to drunken parties, or take part in any other evil activity, regardless of who else may be doing it. In other words, we should avoid all occasions that are *certainly* sinful.

While we can be influenced by others, it is also true that we can influence others through our own behavior. The world desperately needs saints to lead it to the truth of the Catholic Faith. If we do not tell others about the Faith (by our words and actions), who will? The Catholic Faith is a revealed religion and therefore not something we are born knowing, or come to know through reason alone. We have not given the Faith to ourselves; we have received it from others, and we must in turn share it with others.

This can be done in simple ways, like sharing a good Catholic book with someone; asking for someone's prayers (this is good not only for you, but for the person you ask, as it will remind and encourage him to pray in general); writing to an elected official about a matter concerning the Faith (maybe a pro-life issue), etc. In sharing the Faith with others, it must be remembered that it is not necessary to teach the entire catechism to everyone we meet—doing small things with a good intention is all that is needed.

Saint Thérèse of Lisieux (1873-1897), the saint of simplicity, says, "The least act of pure love is worth more for God and the Church than all other good works put together." Let us imitate Saint Thérèse's simplicity and do small things with a pure intention, rather than trying to do many things all at once.

Chapter Two:

Let Go and Let God

Anxiety is the soul's greatest enemy, sin only excepted.
Therefore, above all else, calm and compose your mind,
gently and quietly pursue your aim.

—Saint Francis de Sales

Saint Francis de Sales makes the bold statement that "Anxiety is the soul's greatest enemy, sin only excepted." Of all things that can harm the soul, sin is the only one that does more damage than anxiety. Anxiety drains our faith, hope, and charity, because we are drawn to close ourselves off from God and our neighbor, focusing only on the object of our anxiety, with tunnel vision. Indeed, anxiety is incompatible with Christian humility. He who is truly humble has no need to worry over anything.

Anxiety is wanting to attain something—either the absence of an evil, or the presence of a good—to an excessive degree. It can include wanting to be free of temptations, or wanting to have peace of mind, too much. As we shall see in the next chapter,

Martin Luther was desperate for peace of mind, and this very desperation made peace of mind an impossibility for him.

Having peace of mind is a good and desirable thing, yet in order to have it, one must not want it too badly. In fact, by definition, the very wanting of something too badly demonstrates a lack of peace. Peace of mind is more a decision of the will than an outcome. It results from accepting everything as it happens, knowing that God's Providence extends to all times and all situations. While we cannot control most things outside of us, we can control our response to those things.

Saint Francis de Sales explains, "Anxiety stems from an ill-regulated desire to be delivered from the evil we experience, or to acquire the good to which we aspire; nevertheless, nothing aggravates evil and hinders good so much as anxiety and worry." Like a bird caught in a net, the more it struggles to free itself, the more entangled it becomes. Our desire for something, whether it be security, happiness, or a clean house, can become so intense and disordered that fear overtakes us and prevents us from getting what we are so intent upon getting in first place.

On the other hand, if we moderate our desire for something, we actually become more likely to get it, and more open to the fact that even if we do not get it, there are better things for us out there. Saint Teresa of Avila (1515-1582) says something that may seem odd at first, but which the scrupulous will recognize as true: "Oh, how much we gain if we have no desire to gain what seems to us best and so have no fear of losing [it], since God never permits a truly mortified person to lose anything except when such loss will bring him greater gain!"

Similarly, Saint Philip Neri (1515-1595) explains that,

> God in His infinite goodness sometimes sees fit to test our courage and love by depriving us of the things which it seems to us would be advantageous to our souls; and if He finds us earnest in their pursuit, yet humble, tranquil and resigned to do without them if He wishes us to, He will give us more blessings than we should have had in the possession of what we craved.

In light of this truth, Saint Francis de Sales advises us on starting a course of action, saying,

> If you earnestly desire to be delivered from some evil, or to attain some good, above all things calm and tranquilize your mind, and compose your judgment and will; then quietly and gently pursue your aim, adopting some suitable means with some method.

We should exercise due diligence in carrying out our duties in life, but we never gain anything by worrying over what went wrong in the past, or what might go wrong in the future. If something did not work out, it did not work out. Period. Let us be faithful and move on. Saint Alphonsus says,

> He, who undertakes a thing solely for the glory of God, is not troubled at all, though his undertaking may fail of success; for, in truth, by working with a pure intention, he has already gained his object, which was to please Almighty God.

If we truly wish to please God, we will rest secure in this good will, and not be troubled by outward results that are contrary to expectations.

We would do well to read and take to heart these words from Proverbs: "Have confidence in the Lord with all thy heart, and lean not upon thy own prudence. In all the ways think on him: and he will direct thy steps" (Prov. 3:5–6). When we distrust our own judgment, we are then open to God really working through us. Saint Vincent de Paul (1581–1660) says, "Distrust of your own capacity is the foundation for the right sort of confidence in God." Indeed, if we were entirely self-sufficient, what need would we have of God? Our confidence in Him is based on our humble acceptance of the reality that we cannot do it on our own, and that we need His help.

Let us call to mind and rely on the Providence of God, regardless of the fears that may assail us. Saint Pio of Pietrelcina (1887–1968) says, "Let the world turn topsy-turvy, everything be in darkness. God is with you." Saint Vincent de Paul agrees, saying: "Free your mind from all that troubles you; God will take care of things." Saint Francis de Sales, in his characteristically peaceful manner, echoes the sentiments of these saints, saying,

> Do not look forward to what may happen tomorrow. The same eternal Father who cares for you today will take care of you tomorrow and every day of your life. He will either shield you from suffering, or He will give you unfailing strength to bear it. Be at peace, then, and put aside all anxious thoughts and imaginations.

Chapter Three:

Two Ways
Are Set Before You

All our exertions are of little use, if we do not give up entirely
all trust in ourselves, and place it altogether in God.

—Saint Teresa of Avila

There are two basic ways to deal with scrupulosity: the way of the devil and the way of God. The way of the devil is the way of pride: trying to do it all on our own instead of relying on God's grace, and being one's own final authority instead of relying on Our Lord's authoritative Church. Those who think they are above the authority of God will soon find themselves below even their fellow man. ". . . Whoever exalts himself shall be humbled . . ." (Mt. 23:12). Indeed, Saint Augustine has said, "The devil has been made a devil by self will."

Martin Luther (1483–1546), troubled leader of the Protestant Revolt, suffered from scrupulosity and gave in to the lies of the devil, relying on his own feeble power, and then despaired of salvation. Unable to deal with what he incorrectly thought was Church teaching, Luther heaped his problems upon others by inventing his own religion and scandalously breaking away from the body of Christ.

Luther describes his troubles with scrupulosity in a monastery before his revolt, saying in his *Commentary on the Epistle to the Galatians* (1535),

> When I was a monk I tried ever so hard to live up to the strict rules of my order. I used to make a list of my sins, and I was always on the way to confession, and whatever penances were enjoined upon me I performed religiously. In spite of it all, my conscience was always in a fever of doubt. The more I sought to help my poor stricken conscience the worse it got. The more I paid attention to the regulations the more I transgressed them.
>
> As a monk I thought salvation impossible when I felt the concupiscence of the flesh, that is, an evil movement, whether of lust or of anger or of envy against a brother, etc. I tried many things; I went to confession every day, etc. But nothing gave me relief because the concupiscence of the flesh always came back. Therefore I could not rest, but was ever tormented by these thoughts: Thou hast committed this or that sin, or again, thou art under the domination of envy, impatience, etc. It is then in vain that thou hast entered into this state of life, and all thy good works are useless.

Luther took the cause of his own salvation very seriously. In fact, he took it so seriously that he actually made a mockery of it. Making lists of sins, being always on the way to confession, having a conscience always in a fever of doubt, trying harder with things only getting worse—these are clearly symptoms of scrupulosity, *not* manifestations of the Augustinian Rule.

Interestingly, Saint Thomas of Villanova (1488–1555) was also an Augustinian monk during the same period as Luther. While not at the same monastery, they did live under the same Augustinian Rule, which says in part, "The superior should be obeyed as a father with the respect due to him." In fact, Saint Thomas accepted his appointment as bishop of Valencia not because he wanted it himself, but out of humble obedience.

Saint Thomas was a benevolent bishop who, instead of living luxuriously, gave abundantly to the poor. Among other things, he fed many hungry people, had the town's general hospital rebuilt, established a college for poor students, and had Mass said at early hours so that workmen could attend. All in all, Saint Thomas was a generous man who had a special love for the poor. We see in his life an example of a man who lived happily within the Catholic Church, and we see also that the Augustinian Rule was not, in itself, the problem.

The real problem was the way in which Luther incorrectly understood the rule and, in fact, overruled the rule. Instead of humbly obeying his superiors, he pursued his own path in an attempt to become holy. Luther describes his situation, saying "I prescribed special tasks for myself and had my own ways. My superiors fought against this singularity. I fasted, prayed, watched, and tried myself beyond my powers."

Luther's self-centered attempt at holiness failed, and rightly so, because there is no such thing as a self-centered saint. Saint John of the Cross (1542–1591) says, "The ignorance of some is greatly to be pitied, who load themselves with unwise penances of their devising, putting all their confidence in them, and expecting to become saints by their means." To do this is directly opposed to the command of Our Lord, who said boldly to his ministers in Luke 10:16, "He that heareth you heareth me: and he that despiseth you despiseth me: and he that despiseth me despiseth him that sent me." Our Lord does not want us to go our own way, but to humbly submit to the judgment of our lawful superiors.

It must be remembered that attempting to be holy on our own, without God's grace, will always end in failure. We can do no good work without the grace of God, and cannot even desire to do good without the grace of God. Saint Alphonsus says, "Man is born unable to obtain salvation by his own strength, but God in His goodness grants to everyone the grace of prayer, by which he is able to obtain all other graces which he needs in order to keep the commandments and be saved."

Luther thought that salvation was impossible, not because he looked objectively at the teaching of the Church and at his own actions—far from it. IIe thought salvation was impossible because he misunderstood Church teaching and because he was living in his own self-centered little world, where nothing done was ever good enough. The true teaching of the Church is that God wills the salvation of all mankind, without exception. Saint Peter tells us in 2 Peter 3:9, "The Lord delayeth not his promises, as some imagine, but dealeth patiently for your sake, not willing that any should perish, but that all should return to penance." Saint Paul echoes this in 1 Timothy 2:3–4, saying, ". . .God our Savior, Who will have all men to be saved and to come to the knowledge of the truth."

That Our Lord and Savior Jesus Christ died for each and all of mankind is a basic teaching of the Church, confirmed by the Bible and the early Church Fathers. Anyone who says that Our Lord died for some men, and not all, is in direct opposition to the teaching of the Church. Saint Thomas Aquinas (1225–1274) sums up the Catholic teaching, saying, "Christ Jesus is the mediator between God and men; not between God and some men, but between Him and all men; and this would not be, unless He willed all to be saved." Could the true teaching of the Church be any plainer?

Luther also confused concupiscence—or temptation—with sin, when in reality temptation and sin are as different as night and day. No temptation—regardless of how strong or how prolonged—is in itself sinful. *Only deliberate commission of the object of temptation constitutes sin—there must be full knowledge of the intellect and full consent of the will for sin to occur.* Indeed, we can actually be strengthened by temptations, if we humbly realize our weakness and confidently ask Our Lord for help in prayer.

Because he equated temptation with sin, Luther tried to remove his temptations by going to confession. Of course it is reasonable to desire to be freed from temptation, and there are ways in which temptations can be reduced, such as avoiding clearly sinful situations, consistently praying, and peacefully yet purposefully keeping busy with some good activity. Though it is not the main effect of the sacrament, it is also possible to reduce temptations through the Sacrament of Penance. However, this is a by-product of the confession of *actual* sins, not confession of temptations as though they were sins.

It should also be remembered that we will only be free from all temptations after death. Attempting to remove all temptation by going to Confession is an inherent impossibility, and trying to achieve the impossible will only bring about more distress, which is what happened with Luther. The fact is, we will be tempted throughout our lives, but we never have to give in to the temptations—God always gives the grace to overcome temptations to those who ask for it in prayer. Let us humbly accept the reality of temptations and above all else confidently ask for God's grace to overcome them.

Luther further revealed his scrupulous tendencies when he removed seven books of the Old Testament, books that had been part of the official canon of the Bible since the fifth century. Even some of the remaining books did not fare well either. Luther wrote, "The book of Esther I toss into the Elbe [River]. I am such an enemy to the book of Esther that I wish it did not exist." He also wrote in his 1522 *Preface to the New Testament* that "Saint James' epistle is really an epistle of straw, for it has nothing of the nature of the Gospel about it." If that is not bad enough, read what he wrote in his 1522 *Preface to the Revelation of Saint John:*

> About this book of the Revelation of John... I miss more than one thing in this book, and it makes me consider it to be neither apostolic nor prophetic . . . I can in no way detect that the Holy Spirit produced [it . . . there are many far better books available for us to keep... My spirit cannot accommodate itself to this book.

Notice how Luther bases biblical authenticity not on any objective standard, but on his own personal opinion about the books. If he did not like or understand certain books, then he removed or sharply criticized them. This is another clear indication of scrupulosity, as the scrupulous tend to rely on themselves rather than on the judgment of lawful authority. This tendency can lead to eliminating things that the scrupulous do not understand, such as the Mass, the Sacrament of Reconciliation, or books of the Bible.

Lutheranism, the new theology Luther invented, was his way of dealing with scruples. Instead of humbly asking for help and obeying his superiors, Luther, led by misunderstanding and pride, went to the extreme of changing 1500 years of Christian theology and breaking away from the body of Christ. Starting his own religion with fewer sacraments, fewer books of the Bible, and no authority except his own personal opinion, was Luther's answer to his problems.

Note well that Luther did not try to adapt his way of thinking to traditional Christian theology (which is the goal of every true Christian), but instead adapted traditional Christian theology to *his* way of thinking. Instead of humbly submitting to proper authority, Luther arrogantly followed his own opinions, inaugurating an unparalleled division of the body of Christ.

Aside from the disastrous consequences of his revolt on the rest of the Church, Luther's extreme reaction to God's authoritative Church in no way made things better for himself. In fact, he was unable to make up his mind about the most basic doctrines of the Faith. For example, he changed from belief in the seven sacraments to belief in two, then three, then five.

Saint Alphonsus tells us,

> Luther was constantly contradicting himself: On the single article of the Eucharist, he fell into thirty-three contradictions! A single

contradiction is enough to show that they [the
protestant 'reformers'] did not have the Spirit
of God. "He cannot deny Himself" (2Tim. 2:13)
. . . take away the authority of the Church, and
neither divine revelation nor natural reason
itself is of any use, for each of them may be
interpreted by every individual according to his
own caprice . . . *if you take away obedience to
the Church, there is no error which will not be
embraced.*

One of Luther's contemporaries, Johann
Cochlaeus (1498-1522) said, "The seven-headed
Luther everywhere contradicts himself and his own
teaching." If you want to see the result of a scrupulous
soul not obeying the Church, look no further than
the desperately discontented Martin Luther. As Saint
Bernard (1090-1153) has said, "He who constitutes
himself his own master becomes the disciple of a
fool."

If, on the other hand, you want to see how a
scrupulous soul can get beyond the darkness and live in
peaceful clarity, look no further than Saint Alphonsus
Liguori, who suffered from scruples at different times
in his life. The rest of the verse from Matthew 23:12
quoted above reads, "and he who humbles himself shall
be exalted." This is the case with Saint Alphonsus, who
humbly obeyed his superiors and is now recognized as
one the greatest saints of the Church.

Saint Alphonsus was born near Naples, Italy, in
1696, the oldest of eight children. Because his father
was often away at sea as a navy captain, his mother
was the main influence on him during these times.
His mother struggled with scrupulosity, which she
apparently passed on to Saint Alphonsus through
a very rigorous devotion. During his studies at the

University of Naples, he was further influenced by a professor who endorsed a very rigid moral theology, a theology which, on the surface, seemed admirable and safe, but which was in fact deeply flawed and therefore not conducive to attaining peace of mind.

Saint Alphonsus saw sin everywhere, and lived in great fear of being lost. He had been taught to "play it safe" by always choosing the more rigorous opinion in any given situation. However, he came to recognize that, *in theory*, this rigid way of doing things was safer; yet, *in reality*, having freedom in doubt was much safer. Always "playing it safe" only creates requirements where they did not exist before. The freeing concept is that we are certainly required to avoid *certain* sin; we are not required to avoid what *might be* sin. This will be explained more in Chapter Five.

Saint Alphonsus also learned that humble obedience to his lawful superiors would bring peace of mind and true wisdom. He knew this was the way of the saints, and practiced it so well that he became one of them. Even after being ordained a bishop, Saint Alphonsus still obeyed his spiritual director. In the preface to his book *The Passion and Death of Jesus Christ,* published when he was nearing eighty years of age, Saint Alphonsus writes,

> In my book *The Glories of Mary*, I promised to write for you ⌊the reader⌋ another ⌊book⌋ that should treat of the love of Jesus Christ; but on account of my corporal infirmities, my director would not permit me to keep my promise.

What remarkable words coming from a bishop! The great saint, even as a bishop, obeyed his spiritual director, rather than his own inclinations. This was no small matter about which he was obeying; it was regarding his public promise to publish a book. In other words, he had told people publicly he would do something, and yet, because his director told him not to do it, he did not do it. Saint Alphonsus obeyed his director as a child would obey his father.

Many other saints have been afflicted by scruples at times, but they all persevered by relying on the grace of God, and are now officially recognized as being among those who see God face to face in Heaven. One of the major means the saints used to overcome scrupulosity is humble obedience to a spiritual director (which we will study more closely in Chapter Sixteen). The other major means is to live out the concept of liberty in doubt (explored further in Chapter Five).

Chapter Four:

Staying in the Church

. . . no matter where man looks, no matter how he strives, if he wanders far from God, he will not enjoy nature's tranquility, which he seeks, nor harmony and peace of soul. . .

—Pope Pius XII (1939–1958)

In order to better understand the nature of scrupulosity, it is useful to step back and take an objective look at things. What can be seen is this: a sincere, serious soul wants to do what is best—serving God and becoming a saint. This desire is a great step toward holiness, a step that not too many people take. Satan sees this and is greatly troubled, because he does not want another saint.

An insincere or careless soul is no threat to Satan, so he sometimes leaves it in a sort of fog, which some may describe as "peace" but is, in fact, more like a drugged state. Leaving these souls in a kind of lethargy, he spends his time on those who are in, and those who are about to be in, a state of grace. Saint John Vianney (1786-1859) tells us, "The devil only tempts those souls who wish to abandon sin and those in a state of grace. The others belong to him; he has no need to tempt them."

Satan wants us to leave the Church with the false hope of finding happiness—we can only be tempted to do something that is an apparent good. However, this apparent good of happiness outside the Church is in fact an illusion. We may find some relief for a period of time, but ultimately, leaving the Church will result in more pain and confusion. This is clearly demonstrated in the case of Martin Luther, seen in Chapter Three.

The most fundamental method through which Satan tries to get us out of the Church is attempting to convince us to sin. When someone commits sin, especially grave sin, it becomes easier to leave the Church. Everyone knows that a man's beliefs influence his actions, yet what is also true is that a man's actions influence his beliefs. There is a saying that it is easier to act yourself into a way of believing than to believe yourself into a way of acting.

For example, if someone steals from his employer, it might be easier for him to mentally toss out the Seventh Commandment rather than stop stealing, confess his sin, make amends, and remain in the Church. After one commandment is removed, it is easier for the others to be removed; with the result that one no longer sees the importance of the Church and actually leaves the Church behind. In this case, the man's sins have blinded him to the truth. He claims the Church is not for him, based on this or that reason, but the real reason is the fact that he loves his sin more than he loves the Church.

Unrepentant grave sin is a simple means of being led out of the Church, yet Satan uses a subtler trick for those of us who do not commit such sin. If he does not succeed in getting us to sin, he attempts to make us think we have sinned when in fact we have not. He will try to convince us that God's commands are just too difficult, unreasonable, or even impossible, to obey.

This will lead to confusion and anxiety, perhaps even to thinking that the only way to find peace is by leaving the Church.

This way of tempting us is nothing new. Recall that, in the Garden of Eden, when Satan tried to make Eve think that God was being unreasonable in His expectations of her, he lied to her, saying, "Why hath God commanded you, that you should not eat of every tree of paradise?" (Gen. 3:1).

In actual fact, God had told Eve that she and Adam might eat of all the trees in the garden, except for the one in the center. In other words, every single tree in the entire garden was open to their consumption, excepting only one. This seems very reasonable, yet what does Satan do? He tries to make Eve think that God had put her under an unreasonable obligation of not eating of *any* of the trees.

The same thing happens today when Satan makes us think we must confess all the sins we can think of, or go to Mass every day of the week, or have absolute certainty of having said all the words of our prayers. Confession, Mass, and prayer are all good things, and God has given us certain guidelines regarding them. However, in these guidelines no one will ever find the above requirements. To think that they are requirements binding under pain of sin will lead to us thinking that God is unreasonable, if we do not stop and learn the truth.

What happens with the scrupulous is that Satan attempts to fill them with the fear of those things they need most. The soul fears holy water, Confession, Holy Communion—the means God gives to us for our sanctification. Because God wants us to stay in His Church—"... the pillar and ground of the truth" (1Tim. 3:15)—we can take it as certain that any scrupulous fear of the Church comes not from God, but from Satan, the world, or from our own troubled mind. Whenever we encounter such fears, let us be at peace and remain within the Church, humbly receiving the sacraments and using the sacramentals in order to become more fully united with Our Lord.

This unity with Our Lord is most fully brought about when we receive Him in Holy Communion. In the most Holy Eucharist, we receive the Body, Blood, Soul and Divinity of Our Lord, becoming united with Him in a way so special, that not even the angels are capable of it. Saint Maximilian Kolbe (1894-1941) says plainly that "If angels could be jealous of men, they would be so for one reason: Holy Communion."

Saint Alphonsus tells us further that:

> If you believe that the eternal Father has given you His Son, believe also that He will give you everything else which is infinitely less than His Son. Do not think that Jesus Christ is forgetful of you, since He has left you, as the greatest memorial and pledge of His love, Himself in the most Holy Sacrament of the altar.

Considering this, let us confidently stay with Our Lord, knowing that no matter where we look outside the Church, we will not find true happiness and peace of soul. True peace of soul is only to be found in the Roman Catholic Church, which Our Lord founded for the salvation and sanctification of all mankind. We are all sinners, which is why we all need the Church and her means of salvation. As the saying goes, the Church is not simply a museum of saints, but a hospital for sinners. Let us humbly admit our weakness, and look to the Church for the help we need.

Chapter Five

When in Doubt, It Doesn't Count

An uncertain law cannot impose a certain obligation.
—Saint Alphonsus Liguori

Doubt can be torturous to the scrupulous soul. A challenge presents itself and it seems as if there is no way out. Every direction one looks appears to be problematic and the confusion only gets worse. What is one to do in such a situation where no option looks acceptable? Believe it or not, the answer is always very simple, which makes doubt one of the most freeing situations a scrupulous soul can encounter!

To paraphrase the Redemptorist Father Donald Miller, when you are in doubt as to whether or not you are obliged to do or not to do something, you can take it as certain that you are not obligated, and act without any dread of sin at all. The shorter and more easily remembered version is, *when in doubt, it doesn't count!*

No matter what the situation is, if the scrupulous soul is doubtful about his obligation in it, he can take it as certain that there is no obligation. This applies to whether one is obliged to do something or not to do something. Saint Alphonsus states clearly, "When there exists in a scrupulous person the habitual will not to offend God, it is certain that he acts in doubt and there is no sin." He also says, "Scrupulous persons tend to fear that everything they do is sinful," and that "they should act against their groundless fears."

To use an example: on a Saturday morning you are not sure if you are required to receive the Sacrament of Reconciliation. You feel as though you should go, but when you ask yourself exactly what would be confessed, nothing comes up except vague notions of things that *may* be sinful. Despite this lack of matter for Confession, the feeling of uneasiness persists. What is one to do?

The answer is refreshingly easy: You are *not* obligated to go to Confession! The saying, *when in doubt, it doesn't count* comes into play here. The Latin version is *in dubiis, libertas*, or "where there is doubt, there is freedom." This rule applies even to the holiest of things: the sacraments of Reconciliation and Holy Communion. When a scrupulous soul is in doubt as to whether he has to go to Confession, he can be certain that he is not required to go. When in doubt as to whether he has to refrain from receiving Holy Communion, he can take it as certain that he does not have to refrain (and thus may go ahead and receive Holy Communion).

The principle of liberty in doubt also applies when someone is in doubt as to whether or not he is in doubt. In other words, if someone doubts whether he is doubting or just trying to make himself believe he is doubting, it is certain that he is, in fact, doubting. There is doubt about the doubt. Thus, when in doubt, it doesn't count!

Learning and applying this concept will enable one to bypass the difficulties that can occur for someone in doubt. Doubt not dealt with, promotes indecision. One may be sincere about wanting to do the right thing, yet he thinks that no option is an acceptable one. Therefore, instead of simply choosing a course of action, the doubtful soul remains inactive and worried, which only complicates things further by bringing on more doubt.

Scrupulous souls tend to want a situation to be 'perfect' before they act. This keeps them waiting indefinitely, as there will never be a 'perfect' situation where every last detail is suited to our liking. Of course some situations appear better than others, but having one in which there is no possibility of failure or pain is not ever going to happen. Furthermore, wanting the feeling of perfect security before making a decision will only increase feelings of insecurity. However, deciding to "be comfortable with being uncomfortable" will allow the soul to be at peace, even before a decision is reached.

Additionally, making a firm decision and sticking to it will allow for peace of mind *after* the decision. While it is true that one may need some time to make a big decision (such as accepting a job, buying a car, etc.) putting off making a little decision for an undue amount of time, or making a decision and then changing it (and perhaps changing it yet again) will not bring any relief. As Saint Julie Billiart (1751–1816) asserted, "better mistakes than paralysis," and "there must be no looking back on the past, no anxieties about the future."

Making a firm decision and sticking to it provides strength and brings relief. As Saint Alphonsus said plainly, "A resolved will [aided by the grace of God] conquers everything." Saint Bernard explains, "At first, some [action] will seem intolerable; if you accustom yourself to it, in process of time it will not appear so difficult; afterwards you shall not feel it; and in the end you will take delight in it."

Making a decision involves a certain degree of humility, because in making a decision, one is accepting reality—the reality that only one thing can be done at a time. When someone chooses to do one thing, he automatically chooses not to do many others. For example, if I choose to play tennis, I thereby choose not to go to the store, vacuum the carpet, or mow the lawn. As human beings, we can only do one thing at a time, and when we are doing that one thing, we are incapable of doing numberless others. This is a simple reality of life that everyone encounters.

What can help in getting used to making decisions is to make one at a time, starting with a little one. It may be extremely difficult for someone who never exercises to decide to start walking for half an hour every day. Starting by walking five minutes a day instead would probably be an easy task, but even if the person is in such a state that five minutes of walking is too much, he may simply start with one minute. After this becomes a habit, he could slowly progress further, and eventually would reach the half hour. (For more on this topic, see Chapter Eight.)

We must recognize that what is needed for making a decision is not a perfect situation, but a firm will to do what appears best. As Saint Joseph of Cupertino (1603-1663) stated, "I don't like scruples or melancholy; let your intentions be the right ones. Then don't be afraid." No one, apart from having a special grace from God, has all the information needed to make an inerrant decision. Everyone, whether he realizes it or not, makes "educated guesses" every day. We pursue the path that seems best to us, yet there are no guarantees that it will work out as we would like it to. This should not be a cause of trouble for the Christian, as God requires us to be faithful, not to be successful. A faith firmly grounded in the reality of God is more secure than merely natural, human "certainty".

Besides this, waiting indefinitely for the "perfect situation" keeps the doors open to negative influences, which brings about more trouble. Saint Ignatius of Loyola (1491–1556) says, "Idleness begets a life of discontentment. It develops self-love, which is the cause of all our miseries, and renders us unworthy to receive the favors of divine love." The saying, "Idle hands are the devil's workshop" is true, and idle minds fare no better. Saint Thomas More (1478–1535) tells us, "Occupy your minds with good thoughts, or the enemy will fill them with bad ones. Unoccupied, they cannot be." How true that is—let us conquer evil with good—that is, with good thoughts and good deeds.

It is easy to get so focused on what not to do that we can partially or even entirely forget what we should be doing. God does not call us only to give up sin, but to be virtuous. It is not enough to refrain from doing bad; we must also do good, and one of the great things about doing good is that by definition, we are automatically not doing bad. We must, as human beings, keep our attention on something. It is simply not possible to refrain from doing or thinking anything, as if we could go to a place of non-existence, in order to avoid evil. So, let us keep our attention on good things, developing healthy thoughts and deeds.

When our minds are full of good thoughts, it is much easier to do good things. Not that we must of necessity have a well-filled mind before doing anything good, but doing good becomes much easier. One of the areas in which this is true is that of images. Of course we should avoid inappropriate images, but let us also take in good images. Indeed, if we do not replace a bad mental image with a good one (or what some would call indifferent, such as a tree, flower, door, table, etc.), what are we supposed to replace it with?

We can sit in a church, for example, and enjoy a scene from a stained glass window, taking in the beauty of the particular portrayal of a sacred event before us. It is not merely a matter of simply glancing at it, but really taking a few minutes to appreciate the colors and symbols used, letting it make an impression on us. This can be done with one picture at a time, and we will eventually develop a mental file of pleasant scenes that can be focused on, even when we are not physically present before the actual picture.

In addition to the visual route just mentioned, we can also develop good thoughts verbally. Let us make acts of faith, hope, and charity not only mentally, but verbally, as if we had no doubt about them. It is easier to push unwanted thoughts out of the mind by verbally affirming contrary thoughts, rather than merely thinking them. For example, if there is a thought of despair of salvation that does not seem to leave, let us make an act of hope out loud. It should be noted that hope is not merely a feeling, but a conviction, and according to Saint Thomas Aquinas, hope is the certain expectation of beatitude.

Depending one's specific situation, getting rid of unwanted thoughts can also be done by physically doing something. This of course is not always possible, or even necessary, but it can be beneficial when one has the chance to do it. If one is at home and has been sedentary for a while, and bad thoughts present themselves to his mind, he can, in addition to praying, get up and take out the garbage, get the mail, weed the garden, or do some other physical activity.

In our desire to find the perfect situation in which we avoid all suffering, let us remember the words of Blessed Sebastian Valfré (1629–1710): "Life without a cross is the heaviest cross of all." And why is this so? Emptiness opens the door to the lies of the devil. Let us keep our minds filled with good thoughts and our bodies occupied with good actions so that we will not be prey to the silly fears the devil would otherwise cast upon us. So let us not run from, but accept, the reality immediately before us and do the best we can prayerfully do with it.

Doing the best we can includes living out the life-changing concept of liberty in doubt, which frees us from groundless fears and enables us to live strong, virtuous lives. Nagging doubts that once plagued us and held us back from doing good things, are now relegated to the class of things we consider unimportant, things that we can laugh at. After doing so, we can confidently make decisions and follow through on them.

If you are certain something is sinful, then certainly refrain from doing it. If, however, you are in doubt as to the sinfulness of an action, remember that there is liberty in doubt and therefore no obligation is present. What is present is freedom: *In dubii, libertas.* When in doubt, it doesn't count!

Chapter Six:

Behold
Your Mother, Mary

Go to Mary, and you will be saved.

—Saint Bernard

When Our Lord was dying on the Cross—the most solemn moment of His Life—He gave us His mother Mary to be our mother as well. We read in Saint John's Gospel, "When Jesus therefore had seen his mother and the disciple standing whom he loved, he saith to his mother: Woman, behold thy son. After that, he saith to the disciple: Behold thy mother. And from that hour, the disciple took her to his own." (Jn. 19:26–27).

Our Lord gives His disciples over to His mother as her spiritual children, and He gives her to us as our spiritual mother. The text in the Gospel does not mention Saint John's name; he is simply described as "the disciple" so what Our Lord says here is *directed to all of His disciples*, not only Saint John. This scene shows us that Our Lord gives Mary to us as our spiritual mother, through whom we receive all the graces of His passion, death, and resurrection.

Mary, the mother of Christ, and mother of all Christians, helps us to know, love, and serve her Son better than any other saint. Unlike devotion to other saints who can help us with specific needs, but not with every need, devotion to Mary is morally necessary (though strictly speaking, not absolutely necessary) for salvation. This is so because Mary obtains for us all the graces we need through her intercession. As it was the will of the Father that His Son should come to us through Mary, it is also the will of the Father that all graces be received through her.

Saint Louis de Montfort (1673–1716) in his great book *True Devotion to Mary*, tells us, "The prayer of the humble Mary, that worthy Mother of God is more powerful with His Majesty than all the prayers and intercessions of all the angels and saints both in Heaven and on earth." Saint Louis further declares, "When Mary has struck her roots in a soul, she produces there marvels of grace, which she alone can produce, because she alone is the fruitful Virgin who never has had, and never will have, her equal in purity and fruitfulness."

Mary knows, better than any individual saint, and in fact all the other saints combined, how to overcome the temptations and lies of Satan. Not surprisingly, this causes him to fear Mary more than any other saint, and more than all the other saints combined. Satan goes out of his way to make people think they can be holy without Mary, because he knows that it is only by Mary that we can be truly holy—that is, pleasing to God, whose will it is that all graces should pass through her hands. The same hands that held the Son of God (who is also her son and God) also hold out to us innumerable graces for our sanctification.

Mary accepted and carried out God's will perfectly, and in doing so she won by her humble obedience what Eve had lost by her proud disobedience. What has Mary won that Eve had lost? Nothing other than divine grace—a share in the life of the Holy Trinity for our souls—and she has won this for all mankind. What remains is for us to ask her to share it with us, and she certainly will.

On a natural level, what love is more devoted than that of a mother for her child? A mother constantly looks after and cares for her child, anticipating his every need, and gives him everything necessary to sustain life. Mary's generosity far surpasses that of a natural mother, and indeed of all natural mothers put together. Saint Alphonsus says, "The Blessed Mother is infinitely inferior to God, but immensely superior to all other creatures. And, just as it is impossible to find another son more wonderful than Jesus, so it is impossible to find another mother more wonderful than Mary."

In this light, it is easy to see how much she would want what is truly best for her spiritual children—a living relationship with God. Any good mother wants her children to love their father, and Mary goes far beyond being a good mother; she is in fact the best mother anyone could ever have. Therefore, let us, in the words of Saint Francis de Sales, "Run to her, and as her little children, cast ourselves into her arms with a perfect confidence."

Mary's intercession will lead the scrupulous from confusion to clarity, as she knows the will of God more clearly than any other saint. Mary lived in the closest union with Our Lord—she carried Him in her womb for nine months, fed Him, clothed Him, and taught Him as her true son. Surely she knows better than any other human being the mind of God.

Saint Alphonsus points out. "Mary is the mother who gives birth to holy hope in our hearts, not to the vain and transitory goods of this life, but of the eternal rewards of Heaven." Similarly, Saint Louis says boldly, "When the Holy Ghost has found Mary in a soul, He flies there. He enters there in His fullness; He communicates Himself to that soul abundantly." If we want life in abundance, as Our Lord wants for us (Jn. 10:10), then we must pray to Mary. It is then that we will be led on the path to truly abundant life.

Let us not be overcome with fear at our sins, but gain confidence from Mary's desire to see us united with her divine Son. Saint Bridget of Sweden (1303–1373) declares, "There is no sinner in the world, however much he may be at enmity with God, who does not return to Him and recover His grace, if he has recourse to [Mary] and asks her assistance." Saint Basil the Great (329–379) says to us, "O sinner, be not discouraged, but have recourse to Mary in all your necessities. Call her to your assistance, for such is the divine will that she should help in every kind of necessity."

Pope Saint Pius X (1903–1914) proclaims, "Let the storm rage and the sky darken—not for that shall we be dismayed. If we trust as we should in Mary, we shall recognize in her, the Virgin Most Powerful, 'who with virginal foot did crush the head of the serpent'." Saint Alphonsus also encourages us to call upon Mary for help, saying, "In danger of sinning, when assailed by temptations, when doubtful as to how you should act, remember that Mary can help you, and if you call upon her, she will instantly help you."

FROM SATANIST TO SAINT

To see an example of the awesome power of the prayers of Mary, let us look at the life of Blessed Bartolo Longo (1841–1926). Blessed Bartolo grew up Catholic, yet left the Church as a young man. He publicly criticized the Church, then became an atheist, and finally lost all decency whatsoever by becoming a satanic priest. Deliberate, open, obstinate worship of Satan and persecution of the Roman Catholic Church was what occupied Bartolo's time. Is there anything more outwardly evil than being a satanic priest? Can anyone get any closer to Hell in this life than by being a satanic priest?

Yet Our Lord in His great patience did not give up on Bartolo. After a time of intense unhappiness, Bartolo felt God's call to come back home, prompting him to leave Satanism and be reconciled to Our Lord and His Church. However, he was so laden with guilt and torment from demons that he almost despaired of ever being a practicing Catholic again. How did Bartolo get back into the Church and lead a holy life? By the intercession of the Blessed Virgin Mary! Through Mary's prayers, Bartolo was introduced to a Dominican priest named Alberto Radente. Father Radente became his spiritual director and helped him out of his deep confusion in Satanism.

Father Radente advised Bartolo, "If you are looking for salvation, propagate the Rosary. It is the promise of Mary. He who propagates the rosary shall be saved." Bartolo followed his director's advice by propagating the rosary in Italy and he was indeed saved. In his last will, Bartolo wrote, "I wish to die a true Dominican tertiary in the arms of the Queen of the Rosary with the assistance of my holy Father Saint Dominic and of my mother Saint Catherine of Siena." Bartolo did in fact die like a good Dominican, and was beatified by Pope John Paul II (1978–2005) in 1980.

The power of Mary's intercession knows no bounds; in truth, Blessed Bartolo says, "The Rosary could very well be called the poem of human redemption." Let us devoutly recite this poem of human redemption, this poem of our salvation, and let us propagate this same poem as well as we can. Saint Louis de Montfort says "The greatest saints shall be the most assiduous in praying to our Blessed Lady, and in having her always present as their perfect model for imitation and their powerful aid for help." Let us confidently call upon the mother of Christ and our mother, because her prayers obtain all graces.

> Hail Mary, full of grace, the Lord is with thee,
> Blessed art thou amongst women,
> And blessed is the fruit of thy womb, Jesus.
> Holy Mary, Mother of God, pray for us sinners,
> Now, and at the hour of our death. Amen.

In our prayers to Mary, let us also remember her most chaste spouse, Saint Joseph, who was closer to her in virtue than any other saint. It is true that Saint Peter was the Vicar of Christ on earth, yet Saint Joseph was Vicar of God the Father on earth. Imagine the humility it took for him to be the earthly father of the Son of God! How humble, how pure, how strong, how faithful, how industrious, how serene is Saint Joseph.

Mary has revealed to Saint Bridget of Sweden that Saint Joseph "was perfectly conformed to the divine will and so resigned to the dispositions of Heaven that he ever repeated, 'May the will of God ever be done in me!'" Saint Teresa of Avila wanted to persuade all men to be devoted to Saint Joseph, because she knew "by long experience what blessings he can obtain for us from God." The Spanish saint further reveals that she has "never known anyone who was truly devoted to him and honored him by particular services who did not advance greatly in virtue: for he helps in a special way those souls who commend themselves to him."

Saint Peter Julian Eymard (1811–1868) says of Saint Joseph,

> Words cannot express the perfection of his adoration. If Saint John leaped in the womb at the approach of Mary, what feelings must have coursed through Joseph during those six months when he had at his side and under his very eyes the hidden God! No one can describe the adoration of this noble soul.

The French saint further states,

> Saint Joseph adored Our Lord in His hidden life and in His passion and death; he adored in advance the Eucharistic Christ in His tabernacles. Among the graces which Jesus gave to His foster-father—and He flooded him with the graces attached\ to every one of His mysteries—is that special to an adorer of the Blessed Sacrament. That is the one we must ask of Saint Joseph. Have confidence, strong confidence, in him. Take him as the patron and the model of your life of adoration.
>
> In no better way can we enter into the heart of Our Lord than through Saint Joseph. Jesus and Mary are eager to pay the debts which they owe him for his devoted care of them, and their greatest pleasure is to fulfill his least desire. Let him, then, lead you by hand into the interior sanctuary of Jesus Eucharistic.

Saint Thomas Aquinas (1225–1274) tells us, "Some saints are privileged to extend to us their patronage with particular efficacy in certain needs, but not in others; but our holy patron Saint Joseph has the power to assist us in all cases, in every necessity, in every undertaking."

> O glorious Saint Joseph, spouse of the
>   Immaculate Virgin,
> Obtain for me a pure, humble, and charitable
>   mind
> And perfect resignation to the divine will.
> Be my guide, father, and model through life,
> That I may merit to die as thou didst die, in the
>   arms of Jesus and Mary. Amen.

No human being was ever more devoted to Jesus and Mary, so we should take Saint Joseph as our model of devotion to them. In our prayers, let us also keep in mind that Mary always leads us to her son. The goal of all devotion to Mary is union with her son. When we honor her, we honor her son, as Saint Louis tells us:

> The more we honor the Blessed Virgin, the more we honor Jesus Christ, because we honor Mary only that we may more perfectly honor Jesus, since we go to her only as the way by which we are to find the end we are seeking, which is Jesus.

Chapter Seven:
Humility
and Simplicity

The most powerful weapon to conquer the devil is humility. For, as he does not know at all how to employ it, neither does he know how to defend himself from it.

—Saint Vincent de Paul

Saint Augustine tells us, "If you should ask me what is the way of God, I would tell you that it is humility. Not that there are no other precepts to give, but if humility does not precede all that we do, our efforts are fruitless." "Humility," in the concurring words of Saint Bernard, is "the foundation and guardian of all virtues." Without humility, we have no desire to pray, no desire to receive the sacraments, no desire to do the will of God in any other area of life. In short, if we do not have humility, we do not have God. In the words of Saint Vincent de Paul: "Let us not deceive ourselves: if we have not humility, we have nothing."

Humility enables us to see things as they really are. If we are humble, we see that we are dependent upon God for everything, that without Him our lives have no meaning, and even more to the point: without Him, we have no life—we have no existence! God holds us in continued existence by thinking of us. If He were to stop thinking of us we would cease to exist. Our reliance on God for literally everything should humble us.

While humility is an interior disposition, it is expressed outwardly in how we relate to God and other men. If we "look down" upon people, are judgmental and impatient, it is quite clear that we are not humble, but proud. Pride is essentially a lie: the illusion that we can do it on our own, that we do not need God, or any human being. Pride is self-deification, and is therefore an abomination to the Lord. Pride begets sin, misery, and death. Saint Teresa of Avila tells us, "The chief object of the devil's work on earth is to fill us with pride."

Pride leads to every sin in the attempt to exalt oneself above others, and even above God. There are numerous topics related to pride that we could discuss, but let us take only one here: that of inventing commandments. While it is a good thing to go "above and beyond" the minimum requirements in life, we must always keep in mind that this is not obligatory, strictly speaking.

For example, someone may want go to Mass every day, and this in and of itself is a very good thing. Indeed, one should go to Mass as often as he *reasonably* can. However, to think that daily Mass attendance is *required* is inaccurate and this misconception may end up hurting our efforts in the long run. The more imaginary requirements we pile up, the more likely we are to think of God as being unjust, which is exactly what Satan wants us to think. (See Chapter Four for more on this.)

We see here an example of how the outward action is not as important as the disposition of the one performing the action. A man who attends Mass daily, knowing it is not required, but doing so out of a desire to grow closer to Our Lord, is far more likely to become saintly that the man who does so out of a fear of being punished for not keeping up with one's own strict standards. The scrupulous would do very well to "get back to basics"—that is, to study the foundations of the Faith and prayerfully conform one's life to them, rather than studying matters of the Faith that have no bearing on one's life, such as the rule of a specific religious order that one does not belong to, all the while thinking one must follow this rule.

Inventing commandments can be a result of pride, in part because pride blinds us to the truth. Humility, on the other hand, is recognition of the truth—first, that God is the source of all good, that we are totally dependent upon Him, and second, that He cares for us infinitely better than we could ever do so for ourselves. Humility also enables us to relate appropriately to others. A humble man obeys his superiors and asks for help when he needs it. When he is wrong, he admits it, and is not disturbed by being wrong, because he does not have an impossibly high standard for himself.

Saint Julie Billiart even went so far as to take delight in being wrong. Not that she intended to be wrong before performing a task, but in looking back on a completed task, she made no effort to hide whatever errors may have occurred. She had once written a letter to a bishop that included some spelling errors, which she would not allow her sisters to correct, because she wanted the bishop to know how ignorant she was. Saint Thérèse of Lisieux had a similar outlook on things, saying, "How happy I am to realize that I am little and weak, how happy I am to see myself so imperfect." How very different our attitudes and conduct can be from these saints—we tend to want to cover up any of our mistakes rather than let them be known, or to admit we were wrong.

Most people do not talk of their mistakes, so it may appear to us that they never make them, but if one were to follow them throughout the day, the perception would be quickly changed. The only person who never makes mistakes is the person who never does anything, so one should never get flustered over mistakes. Interestingly, Saint Alphonsus says, "to be exasperated at ourselves after a fault is not humility, but a subtle pride, as if we were anything else than the weak things that we are." When we make a mistake and get frustrated with ourselves, it is good to stop a moment and ask why we are reacting in such a way. Why, since we are weak human beings, in need of God's constant and ever-present support, would we be surprised at making a mistake?

Is it because we really think of ourselves as above making errors, that we do not really need anyone's help? If we do not think that way, do we act that way? We can be motivated by unconscious forces, all the while not even being aware of them. Saint Alphonsus says, "To be angry at ourselves after the commission of a fault is a fault worse than the (first) one committed and will be the occasion of many other faults."

If we truly want to live more effectively, let us peacefully accept our faults and resolutely try to do better, keeping in mind that a sincerely good intention is worth more than a perfect result. Let us also keep focused on what is before us, rather than on hypothetical situations far away. Saint Philip Neri tells us "A man should keep himself down, and not busy himself *in mirabilibus super se* (marvels beyond one's power)." Indeed, a man does no good for himself or for anyone else by attempting to solve non-existent problems.

On Ash Wednesday we hear the words, "Remember, man, that thou art dust and unto dust thou shalt return." Why should dust glory in itself? The word "humility" comes from the Latin word *humilitas*, or *humus*, meaning 'the earth beneath us'. When we are humble, we are in a sense "on the ground" and we cannot fall off the ground. We see from this that humility gives us security, because there is no chance of falling when we are humble.

Humility lets a man get a clear perspective of himself by knowing his weakness, which enables him to submit to God and to others for the sake of God. Through humility the barriers between God and ourselves are removed, and we are made fit to receive the graces of God. Through humility we realize our need for God, and pray for His help. Through humility, we desire to do the will of God in all things. Humility is a freeing virtue, lifting us out of the mire of selfishness and into the graces of God. As Saint Augustine says, "There is something in humility that strangely exalts the heart."

Saint Teresa of Avila tells us, "There is more value in a little study of humility, and in a single act of it, than in all the knowledge in the world." Why is this so? Because, according to Saint Vincent de Paul, "The most powerful weapon to conquer the devil is humility. For, as he does not know at all how to employ it, neither does he know how to defend himself from it." Jesus Christ definitively conquered the devil, and this is primarily due to His humility. Saint Vincent de Paul asks, "What was the life of Christ but a perpetual humiliation?"

Humility seeks to express itself in action, so that when one saint says humility is the most powerful weapon we possess, and another saint says that prayer is the most powerful weapon we possess, they are really saying the same thing, only looking at two different aspects of it. To be humble means to pray, and to pray means to be humble—they are mutually inclusive realities. The more humble we are, the more we pray, and the more we pray, the more humble we become.

Humility is the beginning of virtue, and from humility all graces flow. Humility prompts us to rely on God for all our needs in life—every aspect of our being is subject to Him. In short, humility is a simple recognition of reality. The humble person simply does what he is called to do in any given situation because he knows it to be the right thing to do, regardless of the approval or disapproval he may receive from others. Saint Francis de Sales says, "We should be motivated by a generous and noble humility, a humility that does nothing in order to be praised, and omits nothing that ought to be done through fear of being praised."

For example, a scrupulous soul may be in the habit of stopping in daily at a church in order to pray. All is well so far, but after a while someone notices this practice and praises him for it. The scrupulous soul is happy to hear the compliment, but soon thereafter feels guilty for his happiness. "One should not do things to be praised, so maybe I should stop doing this," he thinks. Firstly, he should remember that approval of others was not his motive for starting the practice, but simply a byproduct of the situation—a byproduct that was out of his control. Secondly, he is right—one should not do something just to impress people, but it is also true that one should not omit doing something in order to avoid approval of others.

There is a short and telling story from the monk, Saint Poemon, who died around the year 450. Another monk told Saint Poemon how he had a neighbor for whom he did good deeds. However, those deeds were not entirely altruistic, but mixed with self-satisfaction and self-interest. Because of the imperfect nature of the situation, the monk asked Saint Poemon if he should continue to do those good deeds.

Saint Poemen replied in the form of a parable:

> There were two men who had two fields. One
> [man] sowed a crop of corn in which was mixed
> tares (that is, corn weeds), the other [man] did
> nothing. When it came to be harvest time, the
> [first man] had a mixed crop—some of it was
> good, some bad—but he took the time to sort
> the corn from the weeds. The second [man] had
> nothing but useless weeds. Who acted best?

The reasonable man accepts imperfect crops over nothing, and he also accepts imperfect actions over nothing. In the meantime, he should patiently ask God for the strength to do his deeds from the motive of pleasing Him alone, and over the course of time, he will get closer and closer to this goal.

Accepting imperfections is even more important when considering those relatively few things that we actually are required to do, such as attend Mass on Sundays. In such cases, any imperfect motives should be disregarded by the scrupulous and he should simply go forth and fulfill the obligation without any further concern. The more he stops to think about all the motives he might have, the more motives will come up, and the more confused he will become.

We should not expect more of ourselves than is reasonable to do so. Often the reason we are upset at ourselves is because of wounded pride; our lofty self-image has been tarnished by reality. Father Alfred Wilson, in his book *Pardon and Peace*, humorously recommends that the scrupulous soul "try to get a truer perspective on his own importance and realize that his ego is not a synonym for heaven and earth and the whole human race. There are at least a few other things worth thinking about!" Saint Francis de Sales says,

One important direction in which to exercise gentleness is with respect to ourselves, never growing irritated with one's self or one's imperfections; for although it is but reasonable that we should be displeased at our own faults, yet we ought to guard against a bitter, angry, or peevish feeling about them. Many people fall into the error of being angry because they have been angry, vexed because they have given way to vexation, thus keeping up a chronic state of irritation, which adds to the evil of what is past, and prepares the way for a fresh fall on the first occasion.

Moreover, all this anger and irritation against one's self fosters pride, and springs entirely from self-love, which is disturbed and fretted by its own imperfection. What we want is a quiet, steady, firm displeasure at our own faults.

The holy Bishop of Geneva goes on to explain

We can chasten ourselves far better by a quiet steadfast repentance, than by eager, hasty ways of penitence, which, in fact, are proportioned not by the weight of our faults, but according to our feelings and inclinations.

Believe me, my child, as a parent's tender affectionate remonstrance has far more weight with his child than anger and sternness, so, when we judge our own heart guilty, if we treat it gently, rather in a spirit of pity than anger, encouraging it to amendment, its repentance will be much deeper and more lasting than if stirred up in vehemence and wrath.

According to Saint Teresa of Avila, "The humility that disturbs does not come from God, but from the devil." Of course, this "humility" is no humility at all, but simply pride in disguise. Satan tries to make us think it is humble to be disturbed, attempting to disturb us more and more. No kind of anxiety comes from God. One need only exercise due diligence in any given situation; after having done all that we are supposed to do, the results are up to God.

In fact, as much as we don't want to admit it, we do not have control over results. However, when humbly accepted, this truth brings peace of mind. Being humble means accepting everything that happens, knowing that God's providence extends to all times and all situations in this life.

SIMPLICITY

Worldly people hold the virtue of simplicity in contempt. All kinds of extras are required for the worldly. The latest cars, the latest fashions, these and endless other things are seen as desirable—or even necessary—for one who wants to appear great before men. The more complicated or "sophisticated" you are, the better off you are, according to worldly people.

In reality, all complication or "sophistication" does is to invite misery into our souls. The more we complicate things, the more that can go wrong, and the more we get frustrated and confused. We should not make things more complicated than they are, but keep them as simple as possible. Keeping things simple enables us to work effectively and peacefully, having a clear goal in mind. Enduring happiness is not found in trying to impress men, but in doing the will of God, as Saint Thérèse verifies: "True greatness is found in someone's soul, not in their social standing or position."

As Christians, we are called to be simple like little children. Saint Vincent de Paul tells us, "Among those who make profession of following the maxims of Christ, simplicity ought to be held in great esteem." Why is this so? Because God Himself is simple—there is no division in God, no conflict—God is absolute simplicity, perfect in all respects. When pondered over, this makes sense and brings peace of mind. God, being infinitely perfect, is not made up of parts, is not dependent on anyone or anything, and has only one will. According to Saint Augustine, "God is truly and absolutely simple."

Simplicity is closely connected with humility, for when we see things as they are, no false obligations intrude on our peace of mind. We do not exhaust ourselves in search of silly extras; instead, we focus on the one thing that matters, and live peacefully as God wills us to do. Saint Thérèse assures us, "Our Lord needs from us neither great deeds nor profound thoughts; neither intelligence nor talents. He cherishes simplicity." Saint Peter of Alcantara (1499-1562) concurs, saying, "He does much in the sight of God who does his best, be it ever so little." In other words, if you really want to please the Lord, focus on doing one little thing at a time. In doing this, you are doing much

Like the parents of little children, God rejoices not in what we can do for Him, but in the mere fact that we exist. Parents delight in being present with their little children, not for what kinds of things the children may achieve, but for the simple fact that they love their children. Therefore, let us follow the advice of Saint Pio of Pietrelcina, who said, "Walk in the way of the Lord with simplicity and do not torment your spirit."

Chapter Eight:
Big Goals, Small Steps

You aspire to great things? Begin with little ones.
—Saint Augustine (354–430)

One way to help bring about peace of mind is not to expect more than can reasonably be expected from any given person or situation. We can get frustrated when we do not receive what we had expected to receive; if we expect our children never to need correction, or the weather to be sunny and warm in the middle of winter, or our co-workers always to be friendly, then we are setting ourselves up for misery. Let us set ourselves up for happiness by not expecting more than we reasonably should!

One of the temptations of the scrupulous is trying to get everything done at once. This temptation may be followed by frantic, disordered, desperate activity, in a vain attempt to complete everything "by yesterday". Sound nutrition is thrown out the window, sleep is lost, and not much actually gets done, or the wrong things get done, or, in some cases, the right things get done, but for the wrong reasons, and at a great cost— peace of mind. Trying to do too much at once leaves one exhausted, confused, and discouraged.

What is needed in such times of temptation to complete everything at once is to simply sit down and pray. Taking the time to relax and talk with God enables us to see things in the right perspective and then to do them in an orderly manner. We will be able to do small, sane, logical steps—one at a time, and complete them in a persevering yet peaceful manner.

It is okay to have big goals, but they must be put in the proper perspective. No matter how big our goals are, the one and only way they will be accomplished is through small steps, doing one item at a time. There is no other way. Saint Augustine sums this concept up by saying, "You aspire to great things? Begin with little ones."

The greatest saints of the Church were the best at knowing and practicing this "little way". Simply doing a little bit at a time energizes, focuses, and inspires us. Saint Alphonsus says, "The most insignificant action, performed for God's sake, is more profitable than the conversion of the whole world effected from any other motive than the love of God." Intention is more important than the act itself. God does not reward us based on the material greatness of what we have done, but on the purity of the intention in doing what we have done. Put in another way, what is truly great to God is a good intention, not necessarily a grand result.

Small things done, one at a time, will get us much further than trying to do everything at once. The simple saying, "Yard by yard, life is hard; inch by inch, life is a cinch." is very true. It is also true that it is better to get one thing done completely, rather than twenty done halfway. When attention is focused on one thing, it is done better than when attention is diffused in many directions over many things. We should not entertain vain fears about this, that, and the other thing, but keep our attention focused on the task we have at the present moment.

Saint Francis de Sales wanted God to

> preserve us from imaginary fervor that breeds a vain and secret self-esteem deep within us. We are not always asked to perform great works for God, but every moment we may do little ones with much excellent love. "If anyone gives a cup of cool water to one of these little ones because he is my disciple, I tell you the truth, he will certainly not lose his reward" (Mt. 10:42).

And he continues with Bible verses and commentary on them:

> "So whether you eat or drink or whatever you do, do it all for the glory of God" (1Cor. 10:31), and "Whatever you do, whether in word or deed, do it all in the name of the Lord Jesus, giving thanks to God the Father through him" (Col. 3:17). Saint Thomas tells us that these words are put into practice when we have a habit of holy charity. Even if we do not have a designated purpose of performing everything we do for God, the intention to do so is implied by the union we have with God. Every action is automatically dedicated to God's divine goodness. If we are God's children by love, then everything we do glorifies God.

The great challenge for everyone, but especially for the scrupulous, is to lead, as far as possible, a balanced life. The two great extremes found among the scrupulous are idleness and frantic activity. As we saw in Chapter Five, idleness begets worthless fears and paralyzes us, making normal activity very difficult. Frantic activity on the other hand, dulls our intellect and leaves us exhausted long before the day is over. What is needed is balance, as expressed in the Latin phrase, *In medio stat virtus, meaning*, "virtue stands in the middle."

We must work, but not frantically or to excess, and we must rest, but not lazily or to excess. We should ask God for the strength to perform our duties, and then perform them as best we can, with peace of mind and simplicity, doing one thing at a time and letting go of each task at its completion. We do not need to prove to God that we are worthy of His graces by exhausting ourselves over a thousand different things. When we are tempted to do this, let us remember what Saint Thérèse observed: "Little children are as pleasing to their parents when they are asleep as well as when they are wide awake. The Lord knows our weakness. He is mindful that we are but dust and ashes."

Saint Thérèse also said, "Children do not work for a place in their parents' hearts. If they are good, it is to please their parents. In the same way, we should not work towards being saints, but to please God." How true this is. It is a good thing to want to become a saint, yet we need to remember that a saint is someone who loves God above all else and therefore wants nothing more than to accept and to do His Will. Someone who wants to be a saint may end up being a perfectionist, while someone who truly wants to please God will likely end up being a saint. The reason for this is that the focus is taken off of self and directed toward God.

When we want to be sophisticated, even for the sake of God, let us remember and imitate the simplicity of children. In doing this, we are acting in a more honest and effective way than that of sophistication. Our Lord tells us solemnly, "Amen I say to you, unless you be converted and become as little children, you shall not enter into the kingdom of Heaven" (Mt. 18:3). Let us endeavor to become as little children, relying more on our parents (God our Father and Mary our mother) than on ourselves, and let us be at peace with the results of our actions.

Saint Francis de Sales points out, "We always do that quickly enough which we do well." If we are more focused on doing something quickly than well, we likely will not do it well at all. We may even end up taking more time to do it, because of having to correct our hastily made mistakes. The reason for this is that when we focus on things that are (at least somewhat) outside of our control, like the timing of projects, we make ourselves more prone to sloppiness and accidents. On the other hand, if we are focused on doing something well (with a reasonable, not anxious desire), then we are more likely to get it done well and quickly enough. We are able to take things as they happen, putting them in the right perspective and coordinating them in the overall picture.

A simple example is that of reading a book. If the goal is to finish reading the book by this evening—no exceptions—there are two possible outcomes: it will get read in time, or it will not get read in time. If it is not read in time, you will be upset and anxious about it, and may even lose sleep to finish it. This will make the next day start out badly, and you will have a deeper hole to get out of. Even if you do get the book read in time, have you learned anything from it? That is, do you remember the author's main points? Can you remember anything that will help you in life? If not, what is the point in getting the book read by a certain time, just so you can say it is read?

Having goals is a necessary part of life, but we must make our goals reasonable and possible. Setting unattainable goals only increases discouragement, because we are guaranteed of failure. Setting goals that *are* attainable, on the other hand, gives us true purpose and meaning, which is inspiring. We can make little steps along the way to the larger goal.

Perhaps you would like to attend Mass every day of the week. This desire in itself is a good thing. One must ask, however, if this is reasonably possible at the moment. Depending on the duties of one's state and other factors, maybe starting out with attending one more Mass (in addition to Sunday) per week would work best. Once this is a habit, then going to two more per week could be started, and so forth. This way, one can eventually reach the goal of daily Mass attendance, and this attendance would be a stable, firm habit.

Saint Francis de Sales, in his characteristically gentle manner, tells us,

> Undertake all of your duties with a calm mind and try to do them one at a time. If you try to do them all at once, or without order, your spirits will be so overcharged and depressed that they will likely sink under the burden and nothing will be done. In all of your affairs, rely on the Providence of God through which alone you must look for success. Strive quietly to cooperate with its designs. If you have a sure trust in God, the success that comes to you will always be that which is most useful to you, whether it appears good or bad in your private judgment.

It is truly wonderful to want to do great things for God. Not everyone even cares what God wants of him, so to have this care at all is a great gift. We must remember, though, that the God we want to do great things for is the same God who created the universe and established its laws. In other words, in order to serve God, we must do so according to His will, according to His laws. Saint Francis de Sales says,

> The greatest fault among those who have a good will is that they wish to be something they cannot be, and do not wish to be what they necessarily must be. They conceive desires to do great things for which, perhaps, no opportunity may ever come to them, and meantime neglect the small [things] which the Lord puts into their hands.
>
> Our greatest fault is that we wish to serve God in our way, not in His way—according to our will, not according to His will. When He wishes us to be sick, we wish to be well; when He desires us to serve Him by sufferings, we desire to serve Him by works. And this is not because the things we desire may be more pleasing to Him, but because they are more to our taste.

This is a great obstacle to holiness, for it is certain that if we wish to be saints according to our own will, we shall never be so at all. To be truly a saint, it is necessary to be one according to the will of God. In our sincere desire to become saints, we can actually overlook what it means to be a saint in the first place. We can be so caught up in activity that we forget exactly *why* we are doing what we are doing. A saint is one who continually accepts and does the will of God. Being a "saint" according to our own will would only mean making an idol of ourselves, which is certainly not what God wants of us.

The occasions for great advances in holiness rarely come to us, but we can make little steps every day. We do this by accepting all that happens in our ordinary day-to-day lives, following our vocation simply and peacefully, as God wants us to do. Our Lord tells us "He that is faithful in that which is least is faithful also in that which is greater. . ." (Lk. 16:10). Those who want to please God do not want to do many things well; they want to do well those few things God wants them to do.

Chapter Nine:

Suffering Well

When God wills you to begin truly to suffer and sends you what you would most avoid suffering, then you may be confident that you are loved by Him and may hope to see the face of the Lord with joy.

—Saint John of Avila (1500-1569)

Everyone suffers in this life. No matter how evil or how good a person is, he will encounter suffering here on earth. The key difference among us then, is not *whether* we suffer, but *how* we suffer. One can angrily rebel against adversity, refusing to accept that such a thing could happen to him, or he can peacefully accept it, knowing that because of his past sins, he deserves worse than what is presently happening to him.

Saint Alphonsus says,

> This earth is the place for meriting, and therefore it is a place for suffering. Our true country, where God has prepared for us repose in everlasting joy, is Heaven. We have only a short time to stay in this world; but in this short time we have many labors to undergo: "Man born of a woman, living for a short time, is filled with many miseries"

> (Job 14:1). We must suffer, and all must suffer;
> be they just, or be they sinners, each one must
> carry his cross. He that carries it with patience
> is saved.

To the worldly, suffering is seen either as something to be avoided at all costs, or as an indication that we have done something wrong. While it is natural to avoid occasions of suffering, and it is true that we can be punished for wrongdoing with suffering, there is far more to the story, which we will learn shortly from the saints. There are few topics on which the saints write more eloquently than that of suffering, and this eloquence is the result of prayerful, humble acceptance of suffering as a sure means of sanctification in their own lives.

First and foremost, it is important to know that suffering is intended for our own good. Saint Augustine declares, "Let us understand that God is a physician, and that suffering is a medicine for salvation, not a punishment for damnation." Some people think that whenever suffering occurs, they must have somehow lost God's grace. This is not true, however, as we see from Saint Anthony Mary Claret, who stated bluntly, "Great have been the crosses, calumnies, and persecutions which I have had to suffer. All Hell has conspired against me." When you feel the same way, take great consolation from it and be at peace!

Saint Anthony did just this, explaining in his autobiography,

> All disagreeable, painful and humiliating
> happenings I considered as coming from God
> and ordered by Him for my own good. Even
> now as I think of it, I fix my mind on God when

such things occur, bowing in silence and with resignation to His most holy will; for I remember that Our Lord has said that not even a hair of our head shall fall without the will of our heavenly Father, who loves us so much. Furthermore, *God's will in my regard is that I suffer with patience and for the love of Him all pains of body and of soul, as well as those persecutions directed against my honor. It is my firm belief that I shall thus be doing what will be for the greater glory of God.* (emphasis added).

Saint Alphonsus informs us, "If you remember to have previously offended your God and you desire to be saved, you should be consoled when you see that God sends you occasions of suffering." Why is this? Because sufferings patiently endured are a means of atoning for our venial sins, of removing the temporal punishment due to our sins in general, of attaining greater glory in Heaven, and of bringing others back into a state of grace. Why, then, with all these benefits, do we reject suffering so often?

Even that suffering which is a punishment for sin is given out of love for us and is for our salvation. After all, what good father would not punish his son for running into traffic? Would we not all despise the attitude of the father who did not punish his son for running into traffic, or the father who actually rewarded such behavior? We can clearly see how suffering is for our correction and sanctification. The father punishes his son not out of cruelty, but out of love. It is better to suffer for a short time in this life than forever in the next.

Let us read more from Saint Anthony Mary Claret, who explains his love of divine providence in light of earthquakes and plagues:

One day the earth shook five times. I preached a mission in [the] chapel, exhorting all to penance, and telling them that God has treated them as a mother treats her sleeping son: First of all she shakes the cot so as to awake him. If this does not produce results, she begins to shake his body. God does the same with His indifferent and careless children. He has shaken the cot, and if they do not awake He will resort to punishing their bodies by means of plagues, as God Our Lord gave me to understand.

Experience showed that a great number of people went to confession during the earthquakes and plagues who would not otherwise have done so. How true it is that some sinners are like the walnut trees which do not give fruit unless by the aid of sticks. I cannot help blessing God and giving Him thanks for sending the plague upon the land at such an opportune time, for I clearly knew it to be the result of His adorable mercy. It was because of the plague that many people confessed their sins and were ready for death. These [people] God called from life, and are now in the glory of Heaven. Had it not been for the plague, they would have been condemned to Hell forever. But blessed and praised be the goodness and mercy of God, our good Father, full of clemency and consolation!

Perhaps some souls would not even be interested in God's grace had it not been for the plague of scruples. This is not to say that scruples in and of themselves are a good thing, just as plagues are not inherently good things, but that Our Lord can make use of the most painful things for our good, and does so if we allow Him. Let us remember that our true good is

Heaven, that we are not put here to become wealthy or famous, or to enjoy perfect physical health, but to gain salvation for ourselves, and help others to do so. This is what Our Lord calls us to do, and He wants us saved infinitely more than we want to be saved. In 1 Thessalonians 4:3 we are told, "This is the will of God, your sanctification. . ."

So whether a punishment for sin or an opportunity for greater merit and the salvation of others crosses should always be taken as beneficial to us. Saint Philip Neri assures us, "We must accept the adversities which God sends us without reasoning too much upon them, and we must take for granted that it is the best thing which could happen to us."

When we do over-analyze adversities and doubt the goodness of God, we actually increase our suffering. In fact, many times we not only increase our sufferings, but we are actually the cause of them. While outward, objective sufferings (such as being physically hit in the face) are just that—sufferings—it is not usually the outward things that happen to us that cause suffering; it is our own response to such things.

For example, if someone is fired from his job, he is in a sense being handed a cross, or we could say that he is being handed suffering, by God. That man now has two options, and the choice he makes will determine to a large extent just how much pain he suffers. The first option is to get sad, angry, overwhelmed; the second option is to accept the firing (an acceptance that is the fruit of prayer). The first option is the one taken by the proud, who think of themselves as being entitled to things they are not entitled to, while the second option is the one taken by the humble, who peacefully accept opportunities for learning humility. Saint Augustine explains this by saying, "That man is truly humble who converts humiliations into humility."

Let the scrupulous remember that whatever has already happened is out of our power to change, so there is no need to get upset over it, as this will only make things worse in the present. If we truly want to be happy, let us decide to be so, apart from circumstances outside our control. We can be happy and endure suffering at the same time; indeed, the only way to be consistently happy is to endure suffering well, as no one is exempt from suffering in this life. Paradoxically, to accept suffering is to reduce or even eliminate pain; to reject suffering is to increase pain.

Let us be careful, then, of assigning blame for our suffering to outward situations. That is, let us not say "I was doing just fine until it rained," or, "That made me so mad," or, "They made me feel two feet tall." Let us remember to take a humble, objective view of things and not let other people or things control the way we respond to life. Generally speaking, others do not *make* us upset, we *choose* to be upset. Generally speaking, we are as miserable or as happy as we decide to be.

Saint Alphonsus even goes so far as to say, "He who resolves to suffer for God, suffers no more pain." When we accept adversities, they no longer cause us pain, and in fact, they can become great assets to us. There are times, of course, in which we can still feel pain, such as when the adversity is a physical one; but even then, our pain is greatly reduced by the mere fact that we accept what is happening to us.

When we refuse the crosses sent to us, we are not responding well to an outward situation—this response is the cause of our suffering, not the outward event. Saint Alphonsus asks, "What does he gain who refuses the cross? He increases its weight." If we really want to suffer and increase our suffering, then we should reject crosses rather than accept them, as this will only increase our agitation. Saint Alphonsus explains this concept further:

> When we try to avoid a cross that the Lord has sent us, we often meet with another, and a much heavier one. "Only take this cross from me," you say; "another I am willing to bear." Ah yes, but that other cross may be heavier still and you have little or no merit for carrying it. Therefore, embrace the cross that God sends you, no matter what it may be; it is lighter and more meritorious than any other, for you are doing God's will and not your own

Saint Francis de Sales confirms this truth so well in these words:

> The everlasting God has, in his wisdom, foreseen from eternity the cross that He now presents to you as a gift from His inmost heart. This cross He now sends you, He has considered with His all-knowing eyes, understood with His loving mind, tested with His wise justice, warmed with His loving arms, and weighed with His own hands, to see that it be not one inch too large and not one ounce too heavy for you.

Refusal of the cross is refusal to accept what God in His infinite wisdom has given us for our good. God, our loving Father, knows infinitely better than we do, what is good for us. We deny this truth about our loving Father when we refuse the cross. It is easy for the scrupulous to think that security consists in having control over everything, when in fact it consists in accepting and doing God's will. There is infinitely more security in doing God's will than in doing our own.

Therefore, when suffering comes to us, as it inevitably will, let us give thanks to God for such a blessing. Sufferings are indeed blessings, because they lead us securely to God if accepted willingly. Saint Alphonsus Liguori says,

> Even with regard to the present life, it is certain that he who suffers with most patience enjoys the greatest peace. It was a saying of Saint Philip Neri, that in this world there is no Purgatory; it is either all Heaven or all Hell: he that patiently endures tribulations enjoys a heaven; he that does not do so, suffers a hell.

Not only should we avoid making crosses occasions for even greater suffering by refusing to accept them, we must, if we will to become saints, accept them for the sake of God. In other words, we must unite our suffering with that of Our Lord. Let us offer God our Father all our physical, mental, emotional, and spiritual suffering, in union with those of His divine Son. Saint Paul tells us, "I rejoice now in the sufferings I bear for your sake; and what is lacking of the sufferings of Christ I fill up in my flesh for his body, which is the Church" (Col. 1:24). We should make the same offering of our sufferings.

Saint Robert Bellarmine (1542–1621) says, "As in Heaven nothing will be sweeter than to resemble Him in His glory, so here on earth, nothing is more to our advantage than to be like Him in His passion." Saint Philip Neri agrees, saying, "Nothing more glorious can happen to a Christian than to suffer for Christ." When we accept crosses that come to us for the love of God, we give thanks to Him for His blessings. Saint Thérèse tells us that "You will have no difficulty in loving the Cross if you think often of the words: 'He loved me and delivered Himself up for me'" (Gal. 2:20).

Furthermore, Our Lord gives the greatest crosses to his closest friends, as we see at Calvary. His Mother and the beloved disciple, Saint John, are nearest to the Cross of Our Lord. Holiness and humble acceptance of crosses are one and the same thing, as Mary and Saint John show us by enduring the death of our Savior. Our Lord revealed to Saint Teresa of Avila that "the souls dearest to my Father are those who are afflicted with the greatest sufferings." Saint Alphonsus tells us that Saint Teresa appeared after her death to a soul on earth, and revealed to her that she enjoyed an immense reward in Heaven, not so much for her good works, as for the sufferings which she cheerfully bore in this life for the love of God; and that if she could possibly entertain a wish to return upon earth, the only reason would be in order that she might suffer more for God

God is pleased by mortifications of our own choosing, but is most especially pleased by our humble acceptance of crosses that come from His own hand. When someone has taken our usual parking space, when it rains on the day of a picnic, when someone complains to us about something we had worked diligently on—all these things are occasions of pleasing God. We please Him when we peacefully accept that they are happening, and endure them because they are His will.

No matter how much we prepare for a given situation, things often go wrong. When adversity occurs, we should not lose heart, but rest assured that our intention and action matter more than the results. We can have the best of intentions, and the worst of results, but the good news is that God does not measure our deeds by results. It would be completely unreasonable to do so, as results are often completely out of one's control, and at other times, partially out of one's control. Let us take courage, then, and exclaim with Saint Gerard Majella (1725–1755), "In all trials, I will say always, 'Lord, Thy Will be done'."

In the *Catechism of the Council of Trent* we are told,

> As this life is checkered by many and various afflictions, the faithful are to be particularly reminded that those who patiently bear all the trials and afflictions coming from the hand of God acquire abundant satisfaction and merit; whereas those who suffer with reluctance and impatience deprive themselves of all the fruits of satisfaction.

We also read from the words of our first pope in 1 Peter 4:12-13:

> Beloved, do not be startled at the trial by fire that is taking place among you to prove you, as if something strange were happening to you; but rejoice, in so far as you are partakers of the sufferings of Christ, that you may also rejoice with exultation in the revelation of his glory.

Beside storing up merit for ourselves, Our Lord may be calling us to bring other souls into sanctifying grace through suffering. Saint Katharine Drexel (1858-1955) tells us, "The patient and humble endurance of the cross, whatever nature it may be, is the highest work we have to do." Our Lord redeemed us through suffering, and He continues to sanctify us and bring others into His grace through suffering. Saint Madeleine Sophie Barat (1779-1865) says, "Our Lord who saved the world through the Cross, will only work for the good of souls through the Cross."

Let us heed the words of Saint Alphonsus, who tells us to "be convinced that in this valley of tears true peace of heart cannot be found, except by him who endures and lovingly embraces sufferings to please almighty God. The condition of the saints on earth is to suffer and to love; the condition of the saints in Heaven is to enjoy and to love."

Edith Stein, who became Saint Teresa Benedicta of the Cross (1891-1942), expands on this theme, stating,

> Whatever did not fit in with my plan did lie within the plan of God. I have an ever deeper and firmer belief that nothing is merely an accident when seen in the light of God, that my whole life down to the smallest details has been marked out for me in the plan of divine providence and has a completely coherent meaning in God's all-seeing eyes. And so I am beginning to rejoice in the light of glory wherein this meaning will be unveiled to me.

Saint Alphonsus expounds on the providential aspect of suffering by stating,

> This was the end for which the Eternal Word descended upon earth, to teach us, by His example, to carry with patience the cross which God sends us: Christ suffered for us (wrote Saint Peter), "leaving you an example, that you should follow His steps" (1Pt. 2:21). A man held in contempt, and treated as the lowest, the vilest

among men, a man of sorrows; yes, for the life of Jesus Christ was made up of hardships and afflictions.

. . . in Heaven the soul will clearly see all the graces which God has bestowed upon it delivering it from so many temptations and so many dangers of perdition; it will then understand that the tribulations, infirmities, persecutions, and losses, which it called misfortunes and divine chastisements, were all love, all means intended by divine providence to conduct it to Heaven.

Let us reflect that if we be faithful to God, all these sorrows, miseries, and fears will one day have an end, and we shall enjoy complete happiness as long as God will be God. Behold, the saints are expecting us, Mary is expecting us, and Jesus stands with a crown in His hand, to make us kings in that eternal Kingdom.

Saint Vincent de Paul assures us, "Our joy depends on the Cross, and Our Lord would not enter into His glory save by the way of bitterness. He leads you by that same path as the saints." In like manner, Saint Alphonsus insists, "The only way by which we can become saints is the way of suffering." We show our love for Our Lord by peacefully accepting suffering, and we open ourselves up to His great blessings, foremost among them, a higher degree of sanctifying grace, and thus a higher place in Heaven. Saint John Bosco consoles us by stating, "Your reward in Heaven will make up completely for all your pain and suffering."

Blessed Sebastian Valfré concludes this chapter for us by asserting, "When it is all over you will not regret having suffered; rather you will regret having suffered so little, and suffered that little so badly."

Chapter Ten:
Overcoming Temptation

All those temptations to blasphemy, unbelief, impurity, and despair are not sins but sufferings, which, if patiently borne, bring the soul nearer and nearer to God.

—Saint Alphonsus Liguori

Temptations are an area in which confusion about feelings versus the will can occur. The scrupulous can be deceived into believing that because they *felt* a certain way, they must have committed a sin. For example, if someone is insulted and then *feels* angry because of it, he has actually committed no sin. We feel different things at different times, and it is not odd to feel angry at being insulted. Where sin can come in is if someone consciously wills to keep this anger with him, directing it at the person who insulted him. The emotion itself is not a sin; *willfully clinging to it and directing it toward someone is.*

For those who confuse feeling and willing, it is easy to fall prey to the notion that in order to be holy, one must feel holy. Specifically, one may think that in order to be faithful, one must feel faithful, in order to be hopeful, one must feel hopeful, in order to be charitable, one must feel charitable, and so on. In reality, nothing could be further from the truth, as seen by the passion and death of Our Lord. Can anyone reasonably think that Our Lord felt holy while being spit upon, beaten, and murdered? His own words tell us otherwise when he cried out the first line of Psalm 21, *"Eloi, Eloi, lama sabacthani?"* or "My God, My God, why hast thou forsaken me?" Here we see Our Lord and Savior, infinitely perfect in all respects, the beginning and the end of all creation, self-subsistent being, the redeemer of men, feeling like God has abandoned him. So much for measuring holiness by feelings!

Interestingly, amidst expressions of extreme pain and disgust in Psalm 21, such as "I am a worm and no man," (Ps. 21:7) and "They have dug my hands and my feet; they have numbered all my bones," (Ps. 21:17–18) we also see acts of confidence. For example, "You are enthroned in the holy place. O glory of Israel! In you our fathers have trusted; they trusted, and you delivered them. To you they cried, and they escaped; in you they trusted, and they were not put to shame." In another place, "I will proclaim your name to my brethren; in the midst of the assembly I will praise you."

We see clearly from this that what matters is not feelings, but the will. We are called to will good things, not to feel good things. If good feelings accompany a good act, be thankful. If bad feelings or no feelings at all accompany a good act, be more thankful, for your merit in Heaven will be greater.

While we can have an easier time doing holy things while feeling holy, these same feelings can actually become a source of pride, leading us to worship ourselves rather than God. We can become so attached to the feelings that we forget the motive behind the action. Our true goal in this life is not to feel good, but to get past our own selfishness and obtain complete union with the Holy Trinity. This is where true contentment is found. Saint Alphonsus says, "It is of the highest importance to be fully persuaded that the love of God and perfection do not consist in feelings of tenderness and consolation, but in overcoming self-love, and in following the divine will."

Some people doubt that they are really in good standing with the Church, as they do not feel good about certain teachings of the Church. To those who are troubled at not feeling any devotion to certain teachings (or to any teachings, for that matter), and therefore think they are somehow outside the Church, Saint Alphonsus offers these words of encouragement:

> It is sufficient that you want to believe all that the Church teaches without experiencing the consolations of your belief. The time will certainly come when all the clouds will be driven away and you will enjoy the light all the more. In the meantime rest contented to walk in obscurity and abandon yourself into the hands of God's providence and mercy.

God does not require that we feel that the Church's teachings are true. He requires belief that they are true. One can be certain of belief, and at the same time experience no emotional satisfaction with the belief. Therefore we should not be troubled at lack of good feelings when we have the will to believe all that we should.

Saint Francis de Sales tells us,

> Two mistakes I find common among spiritual
> persons. One is that they ordinarily measure their
> devotion by the consolations and satisfactions
> which they experience in the way of God, so that
> if these happen to be wanting, they think they
> have lost all devotion. No, this is no more than a
> sensible devotion. True and substantial devotion
> does not consist in these things, but in having a
> will resolute, active, ready, and constant not to
> offend God, and to perform all that belongs to
> His service.
>
> The other mistake is that if it ever happens
> to them to do anything with repugnance and
> weariness, they believe they have no merit in
> it. [On the contrary], there is then far greater
> merit; so that a single ounce of good done thus
> by a sheer spiritual effort, amidst darkness and
> dullness and without interest, is worth more
> than a hundred pounds done with great facility
> and sweetness, since the former requires a
> stronger and purer love. And how great so ever
> may be the aridities and repugnance of the
> sensible part of our soul, we ought never to
> lose courage, but pursue our way as travelers
> treat the barking of dogs.

The main object of prayer and the sacraments is
to make us pleasing to God, not for us to be pleasing
to ourselves. It can happen that when one is praying
and receiving the sacraments as he ought, he feels a
sensible devotion. There is nothing wrong with this,
and there are definitely good things that can come
of such sensible devotion. It should be pointed out,
however, that this sensible devotion is not essential to

our being made pleasing to God. Saint Alphonsus says, "True confidence in God does not consist in feeling it but in willing it. If you want to have trust in God then you already have it."

Saint Jane de Chantal (1572–1641) says, "To rise above self—this is what must be done—above all feelings, all opinions and dislikes, so that we gaze upon God and bind ourselves to Him by a simple assent." She says of prayer specifically, "The success of prayer depends upon the simple raising of our minds to God, and the more simple and stripped of feeling it is, the surer it is." Lack of sensible devotion can actually be a safer route to go in life than the route of consolations, because then we are focused on the task at hand, and not prone to distractions.

For the scrupulous, who can be deluded into thinking that they may have lost the grace of God, the concept of liberty in doubt again comes into play. Saint Alphonsus tells us, "All the masters of the spiritual life are in agreement that when scrupulous souls are in doubt as to whether they have lost the grace of God or not, it is certain that they have not." When confused about whether we have consented to a temptation, we can take it as certain that we have not, and immediately focus our attention on something else.

There is no way in which a man can be *forced* to commit sin. Saint Cyril of Jerusalem (315–386) tells us, "Though the devil can make suggestions, he does not have the power to compel you against your will." If someone thinks that he has somehow been robbed of his free will and made to commit sin, he can be certain that this thought is a delusion, the object of which is to make the man commit a real sin. Remember the words of Saint John Vianney on the topic: "The devil only tempts those souls who wish to abandon sin and those in a state of grace. The others belong to him; he has no need to tempt them."

In fact, temptations should not be the cause of alarm, as the devil is not capable of harming us, unless we consciously allow him to do so. Saint Pio of Pietrelcina says, "The devil is like a rabid dog tied to a chain; beyond the length of the chain he cannot seize anyone. And you: keep at a distance." Saint Augustine before him expresses the same idea: "The devil is only permitted to tempt you as much as is profitable for your exercise and trial." Saint Teresa of Avila even asserts that "I do not fear Satan half as much as I fear those who fear him."

Saint Alphonsus tells us,

> It is a delusion of the devil to lead some pusillanimous [that is, timid] persons to suppose that temptations are sins that contaminate the soul. It is not bad thoughts that make us lose God, but the consent to them; let the suggestions of the devil be ever so violent; they cannot cast the least stain on our souls, provided only we yield no consent to them.

Saint Pio agrees, telling us, "Remember that the devil has only one door by which to enter the soul: the will. There are no secret or hidden doors." In other words, we have no need to be disturbed at being tempted, provided we do not *will* to consent to the temptation.

What a relief to the scrupulous—no matter how forceful or prolonged temptations may be, they cannot in any way harm us, as long as we do not consent to them. In fact, unwanted temptations can actually become a source of merit for us—we can grow in virtue and grace by withstanding them. Saint Pio says that "when the will sighs under the trial of the tempter and does not will what is presented to it, there is not only no fault, but there is virtue."

This virtue is made possible in large measure due to prayer. Presuming that one is already avoiding clearly harmful occasions of sin and is reasonably mortified (this would include the scrupulous), prayer is the most effective means of overcoming temptations. Saint Angela of Foligno (1248–1309) says, "The more you are tempted, the more you must persevere in prayer." Saint Alphonsus, even more to the point, bluntly states, "If you ask me by what means you may conquer temptations I reply: the first means is prayer, the second is prayer, the third is prayer. Were you to ask me a thousand times, I would a thousand times make the same reply." He explains, "Spiritual masters prescribe a variety of means" for overcoming temptations,

> but the most necessary and the safest is to have immediate recourse to God with all humility and confidence, saying, 'Incline unto my aid, O God; O Lord make haste to help me' (Ps. 70:2). This short prayer will enable us to overcome the assaults of all the devils of hell; for God is infinitely more powerful than all of them.

Saint Vincent de Paul greatly admired another saint who lived in his time, Saint Jane de Chantal. Saint Vincent tells us, "She was full of faith, and yet all her life long she had been tormented by thoughts against it. I regard her as one of the holiest souls I have ever met on this earth." Here we have one saint admiring another, not because she had no temptations, but because she accepted and fought temptations. Saints are not people who were never tempted, but people who overcame temptations through the means the Church has given us. We have at our disposal all the means that any saint ever had (and in some cases, more: Miraculous Medals did not come to us until the 1800s, for example); it is up to us to use them and become the saints God wants us to be.

Chapter Eleven:

Praying to Our Loving Father

He is infinite majesty, but at the same time He is infinite goodness, infinite love. He disdains not, but delights that we show toward Him that confidence, that freedom and tenderness that children show toward their parents.

—Saint Alphonsus Liguori

Scrupulous souls tend to have a very unreasonable image of God, seeing Him as a mean taskmaster or arbitrary dictator who is determined to trip them up. There is no mercy, or even justice, in this God who is full of severity, selfishness, and cruelty. Despite the scrupulous soul's best efforts to make things right with God, he feels that God is not on his side and is determined to see him fail.

The scrupulous soul would do well to stop and ask himself if, in fact, God is much better than this image of Him. The God who brought the heavens and the earth into existence out of sheer, gratuitous love, the God who sacrificed His only begotten Son for our salvation, the God who therefore spares no expense in getting us back home to Heaven with Him—this God is the true God of Christendom, who wills the salvation of all mankind—each and every one of us. He who wills the end, wills the means, and it is primarily through the means of prayer that Our Lord enables us to gain salvation.

Saint Augustine tells us the truth of the matter, saying, "God does not command impossibilities, but by commanding, admonishes you do what you can and to pray for what you cannot, and helps you that you may be able." Everyone has the ability to pray, and through prayer can obtain everything else he needs for salvation. There is no grace that cannot be received through the means of prayer. Saint Pio of Pietrelcina said, "Prayer is the best weapon we possess, the key that opens the heart of God." There is no limit to the amount of grace we may receive, as God is boundless charity. Let us pray with great confidence in God for all the graces we need, foremost among them, those of humility and of charity.

The scrupulous tend to try solving every problem on their own, attempting to think their way out of things, independent of anyone else. Yet the more they think about a particular problem, the more complicated it all becomes, and the more impossible the whole situations seems. The very means selected to get out of the problem—one's own intelligence—becomes a means of increasing confusion. When we rely on ourselves, we open ourselves up to failure. This is what happened to Saint Peter when he protested that he would not abandon Our Lord. Instead of recognizing his weakness and need for help, he relied on his own strength.

Despite the fact that Peter insisted he would not abandon Our Lord, this is exactly what he went on to do. Because he was relying on his own power, he did not bother to ask for help, and this omission left him open to sin. Evil is defined as the absence of a due good, and where else would we get anything good but from God, who is the source of all good? Thus, when we do not pray, we are not filled with good, and therefore leave ourselves open to all kinds of evil.

Notice, however, that after repenting, Peter did rely on Our Lord for help. He did not boast about a high level of virtue, but was honest about where he was spiritually. It does not show up in the English translation of the text, but the original language shows clearly how Peter did not overstate where he was, and Our Lord worked with this sincerity.

In John 21, Our Lord asks Simon Peter if he loves Him unconditionally and without limit, to which Simon Peter replies, that he loves Him as a friend. Our Lord asks the same question, and Simon Peter gives the same reply. Finally, Our Lord seems to accommodate Himself to Simon Peter's weakness, and asks him if he loves Him as a friend, to which Simon Peter replied that yes, he loves Him as a friend. They were both dealing with reality, not with an imagined holiness.

Peter did not assert anything other than the truth. In saying that he loved Our Lord as a friend, his spiritual state was accurately described, and this integrity of Saint Peter left him open for the grace of Our Lord to work in him. There was no pride, no false sense of his own power; he simply told the truth, and Our Lord worked with the little he gave. This little mustard seed of honesty grew into a huge tree of fidelity, capped off with martyrdom—a complete giving of his life to God. Let us take heed of this and not attempt to do things on our own power, but rely on the power of God.

We see clearly in this story an example of God "writing straight with crooked lines," which is a simple description of the making of a saint. A saint is merely a repentant sinner who perseveringly cooperates with God's grace. We start as "crooked lines" and God "writes straight" with us through His many graces. How else can we do anything good but by the grace of God, and how else are we to obtain this grace, but through humble, sincere prayer? Saint Teresa of Avila says, "All our exertions are of little use, if we do not give up entirely all trust in ourselves, and place it altogether in God."

Prayer is recognition of our weakness, and at the same time an act of confidence in God's trustworthiness. Because the goal is not to impress God, we should not let the thought of our sins prevent us from praying. Saint Jane de Chantal says, "We must never dwell on our sins during prayer. Regarding our offenses, a simple humbling of our soul before God, without a thought of this offense or that, is enough. Such thoughts act as distractions." We do not pray well when we focus on ourselves; we do pray well when we focus on God. Saint Thomas Aquinas says, "Our confidence in prayer must not support itself on our own merits, but on the mercy of God and the merits of Jesus Christ." Indeed, if our confidence were in ourselves, what need would we have for prayer?

Far from being angry at our asking for help, Our Lord greatly desires to hear from us. Saint Bernard tells us, "A person who begins to pray, ceases to commit sin," and Saint Lawrence Justinian (1381–1455) goes further, saying, "Prayer transforms men and makes saints of sinners." Saint John Eudes (1601–1680), even more to the point, states that "The earth on which you live, the air you breathe, the bread that sustains you, none of [these are] so necessary to man for his bodily life as prayer is to a Christian, if he is to live the life of a Christian."

All the saints knew the power of prayer. "Great is the efficacy of prayer," says Saint Bonaventure (1221–1274), "for it appeases God, attracts the angels and torments the demons." Because Saint Teresa of Avila knew the great power of prayer, she asserted, "If I could stand on a high mountain where I could be heard by the whole world, I would constantly cry out, 'Pray, pray, pray!'"

God has no need for anything created, as He is perfectly happy by Himself. The reason God has created anything is out of pure goodness; goodness of its nature must be shared. Many things God gives to us without our asking, such as a body, memory, intellect, and will, and even life itself. However, there are some things—namely, supernatural graces—that God will give to us only when we ask. This is not to make life more difficult for us, but to encourage us to freely and humbly move toward a relationship with Him. If we did not have to pray for help, how many of us would still pray?

We do not pray so that God will know our needs; God is infinitely wise and knows all things. We pray in order for us to know our need for God, and to receive His help. God wants to help us more than we want to be helped, and we receive this help through prayer. As we learn to pray better, we will see God more clearly as He is: a loving Father who wants what is best for his children. Saint Jane de Chantal says, "In prayer we must converse very familiarly with Our Lord, concerning our little needs, telling Him what they are, and remaining submissive to anything He may wish to do with us."

Satan will try to convince us that prayer is useless for sinners, and if this does not work, he will attempt to make us think that despite its goodness, we do not have the time for prayer. If even this doesn't work, the attempt will be made to make us think that our prayers didn't "take" and must be repeated until emotional satisfaction is felt. Let us not listen to the lies of the devil, but keep praying. Saint Teresa of Avila says, "I am convinced that the Lord will lead to salvation the soul that perseveres in prayer, no matter how many sins the devil will urge against her."

When tempted to solve our problems on our own, let us remember the words of Saint John Chrysostom (347–407): "It is simply impossible to lead, without the aid of prayer, a virtuous life." If we really want to be strong (the Latin root for the English word virtue means "strength" or "manliness"), then let us rely on the power of God. Saint Philip Neri says, "Nothing helps a man more than prayer," and "Without prayer a man will not persevere long in spirituality; we must have recourse to this most powerful means of salvation every day." Let us not focus on ourselves, but on the great mercy of God, and ask for the help to do His will, and give thanks for receiving that help.

Pope Saint Pius X says confidently,

> My hope is in Christ, who strengthens the weakest by His divine help. I can do all in Him who strengthens me. His power is infinite, and if I lean on Him, it will be mine. His wisdom is infinite, and if I look to Him for counsel, I shall not be deceived. His goodness is infinite, and if my trust is stayed on Him, I shall not be abandoned.

Our Lord will not abandon us, if we do not abandon Him. We must stay close to Him in prayer, cultivating our relationship with Him that will last throughout all eternity.

Chapter Twelve:

Peaceful Reconciliation

You have sinned, but do you desire forgiveness? Fear not, for God's desire to grant it is greater than your desire to receive it.
—Saint John Chrysostom

The sacrament of Reconciliation is commonly seen as a torturous encounter, the intent of which is to produce all kinds of mental anguish. This is a sad misconception, because the sacrament was instituted by Our Lord not for our torture, but for our peace of mind. After his resurrection, Our Lord appeared to the Apostles:

> Now when it was late that same day, the first of the week, and the doors were shut, where the disciples were gathered together, for fear of the Jews, Jesus came and stood in the midst, and said to them: *Peace be to you.* And when he had said this, he showed them his hands and his side. The disciples therefore were glad when they saw the Lord. He said therefore to them again: *Peace be to you.*

As the Father hath sent me, I also send you. When
he had said this, he breathed on them; and he said
to them: Receive ye the Holy Ghost. Whose sins you
shall forgive, they are forgiven them: and whose sins
you shall retain, they are retained. . ... And after eight
days, again his disciples were within, and Thomas
with them. Jesus cometh, the doors being shut,
and stood in the midst, and said: Peace be to you
(Jn. 20:19–25) (emphasis added).

Who cannot see by reading this passage that the
attainment or enhancement of peace of mind is at the
heart of the sacrament of Reconciliation? This is made
abundantly clear by the context of its institution.
In this sacrament, being honest about our failings
before God and man enables us to regain or further
solidify our mental stability. If there is a certain
psychological problem, an instantaneous cure should
not be expected, although it is possible. However,
even without an immediate cure, the penitent will
receive the grace to move closer to mental balance.
We should not be troubled at all about our past sins,
as the very purpose of the sacrament is to have them
forgiven. Remember the words of Saint Joseph Cafasso
(1811–1860): "Heaven is filled with converted sinners
of all kinds and there is room for more."

All the saints were very familiar with the mercy of
God. Saint Frances of Rome (1384–1440) encourages
us to "Hope everything from the mercy of God" because
"It is as boundless as His power," echoing the truth
found in Ecclesiasticus 2:22–23: ". . .We shall fall into
the hands of the Lord. . .For according to his greatness,
so also is his mercy with him." Saint Thérèse expands
on this by stating, "If my conscience were burdened
with all the sins it is possible to commit, I would still
go and throw myself into Our Lord's arms, my heart

all broken up with contrition. I know what tenderness He has for any prodigal child of His that comes back to Him." Furthermore, Saint Isidore of Seville (560–636) explains, "Confession heals, confession justifies, confession grants pardon of sin. Believe it firmly. Do not doubt, do not hesitate, never despair of the mercy of God. Hope and have confidence in confession."

Believe it or not, the requirements for a valid confession are quite simple. We are *not* required to have perfect contrition, we are *not* required to describe our sins in perfect detail, and we are *not* required to confess sins previously confessed. We are also not required to confess in front of the congregation, or to write a book about our sins, or to confess to a bishop (any validly ordained priest with faculties will do). No, the real requirements on our part are very easy—they are contrition, confession, and satisfaction.

Contrition

Of the three requirements for valid reception of the sacrament, contrition occupies the most important place. Without contrition, one would not bother to confess or to make satisfaction. Indeed, contrition is the prerequisite for confession and satisfaction. What matters most is the disposition of the penitent, as God places more value on intent than on outward actions. If we are sincere in our desire to do what God wants us to do (and the scrupulous certainly are), then it does not matter if our outward actions are not performed flawlessly.

What exactly is contrition? According to the fathers of the Council of Trent, contrition is ". . . a sorrow and detestation of sin committed, with a purpose of sinning no more." Contrition is not a feeling, but an act of the will. Sometimes contrition is accompanied by feelings, but it is not necessary to *feel* sorry in order to be sorry. A firm disposition of the will is far more important than fleeting feelings.

Saint Pio of Pietrelcina assures us, "The soul must be saddened by one thing alone: offending God, and even in this we must be very cautious. We must be sorry, it is true, for our failings, but with a calm sorrow while we continue to trust in divine mercy." Just as a deficit of sorrow is not desirable, neither is a surplus of sorrow. To be overly sorrowful is the result of focusing too much on self and forgetting the divine mercy. Let us then humbly accept our limitations, and place boundless trust in the divine mercy, which comes from the God who desires our forgiveness more than we desire it ourselves.

In the *Catechism of the Council of Trent* we read,

> To regulate sorrow belongs to the virtue of penance. Some conceive a sorrow which bears no proportion to their crimes. Nay, there are some, says Solomon, who are glad when they have done evil. Others, on the contrary, find themselves given to such melancholy and grief, as utterly to abandon all hope of salvation. Penance, therefore, considered as a virtue, assists us in restraining within the bounds of moderation our sense of sorrow.

Saint Thomas of Villanova asks, "What do you fear, O sinner, if you detest your sin? How will He condemn you, [He] who died in order *not* to condemn you?" Scrupulous souls are by definition contrite: they are very sorrowful for sins committed, detest those sins, and desire not to sin in the future. Thus, they have the first requirement for a valid confession.

In order to make a good confession, we need to know how we have offended God, which is brought to our attention by an examination of conscience. Most people would do well to examine their consciences more frequently, yet the scrupulous do not fall into this category. In fact, the scrupulous would do well to examine their consciences less often. For some scrupulous people, their lives are nothing but a continual examination of conscience. This is a kind of spiritual vanity—constantly looking into the mirror to see if the soul is okay.

For some scrupulous souls, a vacation from examination of conscience may be called for. However, when the time comes to do so, a good examination should only take a few minutes. If one's thoughts are "hydroplaning" around, endlessly flying from subject to subject, or if there is obsession over one particular item, know that you may simply stop the examination and start thinking about something else.

It can even be a good idea to postpone the examination until one is in the confessional. On the way in, a short prayer to Our Lord for guidance is said, and then once inside, the simple search begins. One mentally moves through the Ten Commandments until it is found that one has been broken, at which time this is stated to the priest out loud. Then one proceeds to the next Commandment in similar fashion, until completion. This postponement of examination can make it easier to cut out silly worries and help bring about a more decisive, firm confession. You may want to try this.

For the scrupulous, great confusion can occur about what exactly to confess. It may come as a surprise, but there is a very simple answer to the question of what we are to confess: *our sins*. We are not to confess our virtues, or the sins of others, or to complain about something going on in the parish. Confession is meant for confessing our sins. More specifically, *we are not required to confess any venial sins, only mortal sins we are sure of having committed.* If we choose to do so, we may confess venial sins, but we are not required to do so. This is quite a relief to the scrupulous, as some labor under the erroneous notion that any and all sins must be confessed.

As for how much explanation of the sins we are to give, we are told in the *Catechism of the Council of Trent* that "Whatever is necessary to make known the nature of every sin is to be explained briefly and modestly" and that "Our confession should be plain, simple, and undisguised; not artfully made, as is the case with some who seem more intent on defending themselves than on confessing their sins." Father Alfred Wilson sums it up well in his book *Pardon and Peace:* "Be blunt, be brief, be gone."

The concept of liberty in doubt should be called to mind here: if you are in doubt as to whether or not you are required to do or not to do something, you can take it as certain that you are not obligated and proceed to act without any fear of sin. This applies to the sacrament of Reconciliation, just as it applies to all the rest of life. If you are doubtful about whether something is a mortal sin, or even a sin at all, or whether you confessed something properly, then the concept applies: you are *not* obligated to confess it.

If you are still uncertain about what exactly to say, simply ask the priest for help. The sacrament of Reconciliation is not meant to be a torturous trial, but an encounter with the mercy of God. The goal here is not to trip you up, but to offer help, so ask for the help if you need it.

Saint Alphonsus tells us that we should not spend a great deal of time in examination of conscience; this is especially the case in those matters that are most troublesome to us. Perplexity, doubt, and anxiety are incompatible with clear thinking, and trying to think one's way out of the situation only makes it worse. What is needed is to simply let go and move on. Father Alfred Wilson is in agreement, saying, "If you are doubtful about a sin, do not spend much time in trying to solve the doubt, because the longer you analyze yourself, the more confused you'll become, and you may even renew the temptation." Knowing this and putting it into practice gives us the freedom to let go of agonizing doubt and be at peace.

One of the reasons why we can get caught up in confusion about whether or not something is actually a sin is that we have made up our own commandments. Some of these homemade commandments for the scrupulous can be, "You shall wash your hands frequently," "You shall be at least half an hour early to Mass," "You shall never make mistakes." Having clean hands, being early to Mass, and being accurate are good things. However, not having spotless hands, only being fifteen minutes early for Mass, and making mistakes, are not sins. Father Wilson tells us "God has given us ten commandments only. If we make additions of our own, we imply that God's way is not safe, which is blasphemous nonsense and implicit lecturing of the Almighty. Let us not make commandments out of counsels."

Even when we accurately recognize something as being a sin, but a venial one, we are able to have them forgiven outside the sacrament of Reconciliation. There is a wide variety of means to achieve this, first and foremost among them, the Holy Sacrifice of the Mass. Worshiping Our Lord at Mass and receiving Him in Holy Communion are ways to remove venial sins. Devout use of holy water, praying the Our Father, genuflecting in front of the Blessed Sacrament, sharing the Faith with another—all these remove venial sins from our souls. There are countless ways to remove the guilt of venial sins, because there are countless acts of virtue we can perform.

Saint Thomas Aquinas tells us,

> Because they imply a movement of detestation for sin, the recital of the Confiteor or of an Act of Contrition and the Lord's Prayer, conduce to the remission of venial sins, for we ask in the Lord's Prayer: 'Forgive us our trespasses' [Such acts] include a movement of reverence for God and divine things; and in this way a bishop's blessing, the sprinkling of holy water and anything else of the kind, conduce to the remission of venial sins.

The only kind of sin that must be confessed is a mortal sin. In the *Catechism of the Council of Trent* we read,

> All mortal sins must be revealed to the priest. Venial sins, which do not separate us from the grace of God, and into which we frequently fall, although they may be usefully confessed, as the experience of the pious proves, may be omitted without sin, and expiated by a variety of other means.

There are three requirements, all of which must be met at the same time in order for mortal sin to be committed. If only one or two of them are met, there is no mortal sin, and one may take it for certain that he is still in a state of grace.

1) The object of the sin must be grave matter (missing Mass on a Sunday or other holy day without sufficient reason, robbery, abortion, kidnapping, or drunkenness, for examples),

2) There must be full knowledge it is grave matter. In addition to the presence of grave matter, one must know that there is grave matter. In other words, one cannot sin accidentally, only with full knowledge of the intellect.

3) There must be full consent of the will in light of this knowledge. One must freely commit the sin, all the while knowing that it is a grave sin.

All three of these requirements must be met at the same time for a sin to be mortal.

Saint Alphonsus assures us,

> It is certain that to commit a mortal sin there must be full knowledge in one's mind and perfect consent of the will in wishing an action which gravely offends God. There is not the slightest doubt about the truth of this teaching. It is held even by the most rigorist of all, Genet. He says that if there is imperfect deliberation, it is only a venial sin and not a mortal sin.

Saint Thomas Aquinas confirms, "What could be a mortal sin [because of the presence of grave matter] is simply venial if the act is imperfect, that is, if the act is not fully deliberate but unpremeditated."

Further still, what could be a mortal sin because of the presence of grave matter may in fact be no sin at all, if the person had no intention whatsoever of committing sin. It is one thing for an action (or omission) to be unpremeditated but partially willed, another thing still for an action (or omission) to be completely unwilled. (For something to be willed, it must be known, and if one is doing something which unknown to him is a sin, this is not imputable to him as such.)

For example, a man is thrown off his normal routine by getting two days off from work. Because of these vacation days, the distinction of what day it is becomes somewhat hazy in his mind. When Sunday rolls around, he does not realize that it is actually the day we are required to attend Mass. Consequently, he does not go to church and spends the day around the house. Because the man had no intention of committing sin, the material sin (missing Mass on Sunday without sufficient reason) is not imputable to him. In order for him to commit a sin (which in this case would be mortal), he would need to know that it is in fact Sunday; that we are required to attend Mass on Sunday; and then deliberately not attend Mass in light of this knowledge.

Saint Alphonsus informs us of something that is extremely beneficial to the scrupulous:

> God condemns only formal sin and not material sin; indeed, so-called material sins are not sins at all. We call them material sins simply because they would supply the matter of sin if such things were done with that kind of advertence necessary to turn them into sins.

This is true regarding what would be mortal sins and regarding what would be venial sins.

Confession

Now that we know what to look for in preparing for this sacrament, let us focus on the confession itself. The second requirement for valid reception of the sacrament is the confession of sin, which is a straightforward requirement; yet the scrupulous can make it very complicated. The Church requires only a good confession, not a perfect one. A perfect confession is not humanly possible; only God is capable of perfectly describing and enumerating sins.

We should also remember that the reason God forgives us is not for being able to recall with meticulous accuracy all the details of our sins, or to describe them in a poetic, precisely worded, and engaging manner. God forgives us because we are sorry for having committed the sins.

In the *Catechism of the Council of Trent* we are told,

> Should the confession seem defective, either because the penitent forgot some grievous sins, or because, although intent on confessing all his sins, he did not examine the recesses of his conscience with sufficient accuracy, *he is not bound to repeat his confession.* It will be sufficient, when he recollects the sins which he has forgotten, to confess them to priest on a future occasion (emphasis added).

Even if, after all that has been learned about the easy requirements for the sacrament of Reconciliation, one becomes so anxious and confused as to be barely able to think clearly, he is not bound to confessional integrity. God does not require moral or physical impossibilities. If, in extreme confusion, one is unable to meet the requirements of the sacrament, he may simply accuse himself of having sinned mortally, without getting into specifics. One should also remember to ask the priest for help if it is needed.

SATISFACTION

Scrupulous souls can become frantic about performing penances properly. What is helpful in other cases is helpful here. Simply sit down for five minutes, take a deep breath, and calmly pray for peace of mind. After the five minutes; or once there is enough calming of the mind, then simply say or do the penance.

We should also remember that penances are not meritorious because of our own efforts; rather, they derive all of their power with God from the merits of Our Lord and Savior Jesus Christ. This is explained well in the *Catechism of the Council of Trent:*

> Of the great efficacy of penance we may form some idea, if we reflect that it arises entirely from the merits of the Passion of Christ Our Lord. It is His Passion that imparts to our good actions two greatest advantages: the first, that we may merit the rewards of eternal glory, so that a cup of cold water given in His name shall not be without its reward; the second, that we may be able to satisfy for our sins.
>
> Nor does this lessen the most perfect and superabundant satisfaction of Christ Our Lord, but, on the contrary, renders it still more conspicuous and illustrious. For the grace of Christ is seen to abound more, inasmuch as it communicates to us not only what He merited and paid of Himself alone, but also what, as head, He merited and paid in His members, that is, in holy and just men.

> For Christ Our Lord continually infuses His grace into the devout soul united to Him by charity, as the head to the members, or as the vine through the branches. *This grace always precedes, accompanies, and follows our good works, and without it we can have no merit, nor can we at all satisfy God* (emphasis added).
>
> Hence it is that nothing seems wanting to the just. Through their works done by the power of God, they are able, on the one hand, to satisfy God's law, as far as their human and mortal condition will allow; and, on the other hand, they can merit eternal life.

We can do nothing pleasing to God without His grace, which precedes, accompanies, and follows our good works. Pope Saint Gregory the Great (540–604) reminds us, "If we do good deeds, we must remember that our strength to do them comes from God. We cannot rely on our own strength." Saint Thomas More concurs, bluntly and humorously stating "The Church has always taught that all our penance without Christ's passion is not worth a pea."

Summary

In summary, we quote at length a passage from the *Catechism of the Council of Trent* that explains the great gift of the Sacrament of Penance so well:

> For each one has good reason to distrust the accuracy of his own judgment on his own actions, and hence we could not [help] but be very much in doubt regarding the truth of our internal penance. It was to destroy this, our uneasiness, that Our Lord instituted the

Sacrament of Penance, by means of which we are assured that our sins are pardoned by the absolution of the priest; and also to tranquilize our conscience by means of the trust we rightly repose in the virtue of the sacraments.

The words of the priest sacramentally absolving us from our sins are to be accepted in the same sense as the words of Christ Our Lord when He said to the paralytic: 'Son, be of good heart: thy sins are forgiven thee.'

No one can obtain salvation unless through Christ and the merits of His Passion. Hence it was becoming in itself, and highly advantageous to us, that a sacrament should be instituted through the force and efficacy of which the blood of Christ flows into our souls, washes away all the sins committed after Baptism, and thus leads us to recognize that it is to our Savior alone we owe the blessing of reconciliation.

How thankful, then, should not sinners be to God for having bestowed such ample power on the priests of His Church! Unlike the priests of the Old Law who merely declared the leper cleansed from his leprosy, the power now given to the priests of the New Law is not limited to declaring the sinner absolved from his sins, but, as a minister of God, he truly absolves from sin. This is an effect of which God Himself, the author and source of grace and justice, is the principal cause.

For there is no sin, however great or horrible, which cannot be effaced by the Sacrament of Penance, and that not merely once, but over and over again.

And Saint John says, 'If we confess our sins; he is faithful and just, to forgive us our sins;' and a little later, he adds: 'If any man sin, (he excepts no sin whatever) we have an advocate with the Father; Jesus Christ, the just; for He is the propitiation for our sins; and not for ours only, but for the sins of the whole world'. The faithful should not despair of the infinite goodness and mercy of God, for since God is most desirous of our salvation, He will not delay to pardon us. With a father's fondness, He embraces the sinner the moment he enters into himself, turns to the Lord, and, having detested all his sins, resolves that later on, as far as he is able, he will call them singly to mind and detest them.

Not less necessary for contrition than the other chief conditions is a care that it be accompanied by entire forgiveness of the injuries which we may have received from others. This Our Lord and Savior admonishes when He declares: 'If you will forgive men their offences, your heavenly Father will forgive you also your offences, but if you will not forgive men, neither will your Father forgive you your offences.'

According to the doctrine of the Catholic Church, a doctrine firmly to be believed and constantly professed by all, if the sinner have a sincere sorrow for his sins and a firm resolution of avoiding them in future, although he bring not with him that contrition which may be sufficient of itself to obtain pardon, all his sins are forgiven and remitted through the power of the keys, when he confesses them properly to the priest. Justly, then, do those most holy men, our Fathers, proclaim that by the keys of the Church the gate of Heaven is thrown open, a truth which no one can doubt since the Council of Florence has decreed that the effect of Penance is absolution from sin (emphasis added).

Let us no longer cower in fear of this wondrous sacrament; let us instead be filled with confidence in the divine mercy. The end of the sacrament is not damnation, but salvation. Our Lord wants us to be holy more than we want it ourselves, and this sacrament is a great means of achieving that holiness. Let us, in the words of Saint Francis de Sales, "Consider all the past as nothing, and say, like David: 'Now I begin to love my God.'"

Chapter Thirteen:

The Theological Virtue of Charity

Charity is the sweet and holy bond which links the soul with its Creator.

—Saint Catherine of Siena (1347–1380)

There are some saints whom it is better to stand back and admire, rather than hold up for imitation. Saint Anthony Mary Claret is an example of one of these saints. He wrote 144 books, preached around 25,000 sermons, confirmed about 300,000 people, and did all this while usually sleeping less than five hours per night, not eating meat, fish, or eggs, and not drinking wine. The scrupulous can read about such a saint and then assume that in order for anyone to become holy, he must have comparable 'stats', as if it is some kind of win-loss record or batting average that we are after, rather than a loving relationship with God.

Saint Catherine of Siena says, "No one should judge that he has greater perfection because he performs great penances and gives himself in excess. Merit consists in the virtue of love alone, flavored with the light of true discretion, without which the soul is worth nothing." God does want us to do good things, but we must remember that good things are done primarily out of love. We are called to put God first, and then the good works can follow. We cannot do any good works without first loving God, because any goodness a work has, comes *from* God.

The scrupulous need to remember that in addition to those like Saint Anthony, there were other saints who, from a merely statistical standpoint, were unimpressive. Saint Thérèse never preached a sermon, never went on a mission, and died when she was twenty-four years old, and yet, she was deemed by Pope Pius XI (1922–1939) "the greatest saint of modern times." Mere statistics are no way to measure holiness!

This is not to take anything away from Saint Anthony, but it shows that each of us has our own unique calling. We are not all called to be ministers of the Church, we are not all called to be known publicly as holy, we are not all called to do manifestly grandiose things. However, we are all called to love and serve the Lord with all we are and all we have. When we do that, the statistics will take care of themselves.

While we may be accustomed to operating on fear, it is not the highest motive for obeying God's commandments. Love surpasses fear, because it replaces a self-centered motive with a God-centered motive. Our desire to avoid evil and to do good is done for the love of God, not merely for the protection of self. The truly secure way in life is to love God and do what He commands for the sake of this love. Saint Robert Bellarmine summarizes it this way: "The school of Christ is the school of charity. On the last day there will be no question at all on the text of Aristotle, the aphorisms of Hippocrates, or the paragraphs of Justinian. Charity will be the whole syllabus."

There is a very close relationship between humility and charity. Humility enables us to see our need for help, which we seek in prayer and the sacraments. The virtue of charity is infused into our souls at Baptism, and we can increase our charity every day through prayer and reception of the sacraments. Saint Vincent de Paul says,

> Humility and charity are the two master-chords: one, the lowest; the other, the highest, all the others are dependent on them. Therefore it is necessary, above all, to maintain ourselves in these two virtues; for observe well that the preservation of the whole edifice depends on the foundation and the roof.

In living out the virtue of charity, we should aim for what God desires from us, not for what is desirable in the sight of the world. We may even be called to do something that appears in the eyes of the world to be a waste of time. This should not deter us, because, in the words of Saint Thérèse, "The least act of pure love is worth more for God and the Church than all other good works put together."

An important part of charity is being patient with defects of others. Most people find that the opportunities for bearing patiently with others are abundant, so it is far better to say a quick prayer for someone whom we find annoying than to harp on their defects. This will result not only in a happier eternity, as each act of charity increases our glory in Heaven, but it will also result in a happier life here below.

This is not to say that we should pretend that no one has any flaws—quite the contrary. We all sin, make mistakes, and have quirks that others find repellant. However, it is one thing to *recognize* this, quite another to be *disturbed* by it. In fact, there is peace in recognizing it, rather than refusing to recognize it, as we see the source of our disturbance in the refusal. We are not disturbed by another's action per se, but by the fact that the other person could have done better and probably knew he could have done better.

For example, many actions performed by a one year-old draw smiles, yet the same actions performed by an adult would draw ridicule and contempt. This is true because the one year-old simply does not have the capacity to know any better, while the adult does. The young child is capable of actions that are unpleasant, or that we could even say are materially sinful, but there is no possibility of intending to do wrong. For adults, there is the capacity to know better, so it is reasonable to expect that they act respectfully and responsibly. However, when they do not act this way, we should accept human imperfection and be at peace. Saint Alphonsus explains,

> Whoever does not bear the defects of his neighbor cannot have true charity. The most perfect souls are not free from all defects. You yourself are subject to faults, and notwithstanding your manifold imperfections, you expect to be treated with charity and compassion. You therefore should [compassionately bear] the defects of others.

While there are times when we are called to carry big crosses, most days we are called to carry little ones. Saint Thérèse shares an initially annoying experience in her own life that became an opportunity for her to grow in charity:

> The practice of charity, as I have said, dear Mother Agnes [i.e., her sister Pauline, prioress at the time], was not always so sweet for me, and to prove it to you. I am going to recount certain little struggles, which will certainly make you smile. For a long time at evening meditation, I was placed in front of a Sister who had a strange habit, and I think, many lights, because she rarely used a book during meditation. This is what I noticed: as soon as this Sister arrived, she began making a strange little noise which resembled the noise one would make when rubbing two shells, one against the other. I was the only one to notice it because I had extremely sensitive hearing (too much so at times). Mother, it would be impossible for me to tell you how much this little noise wearied me. I had a great desire to turn my head and stare at the culprit who was very certainly unaware of her "click". This would be the only way of enlightening her.
>
> However, in the bottom of my heart I felt it was much better to suffer this out of love for God and not to cause the Sister any pain. I remained calm, therefore, and tried to unite myself to God and to forget the little noise. Everything was useless. I felt the perspiration inundate me, and I was obliged simply to make a prayer of doing it without annoyance and with peace and joy, at least in the interior of my soul. I tried to love the little noise which was so displeasing; instead of trying not to hear it (impossible), I paid close attention so as to hear it well, as though it were a delightful concert, and my prayer (which was

not the Prayer of Quiet) was spent in offering this concert to Jesus.

Note well that Saint Thérèse overcame her annoyance *by deliberately focusing on the object of her annoyance*—the clicking noise. This can often be the answer to overcoming similar things: instead of trying to flee, take a deep breath, say a prayer, and be at peace with the situation. Needless to say, this is not always the answer, as sometimes it is more reasonable to get away from something. However, when the situation is not sinful, but merely annoying (such as the one above), then we can peacefully accept it as it is, and in doing this, we gain power over it.

We may be called to do things for people who are looked upon as being unimportant, yet no one is unimportant in the eyes of God. Saint Vincent de Paul says, "We must love our neighbor as being made in the image of God and as an object of His love." When we love other human beings for the sake of God, we love them not for what they can give to us, but for who they are. They, like us, are made in the image and likeness of God, destined to live with Him throughout eternity. Saint Vincent encourages us to . . . keep our hearts open to the sufferings of other people, and pray continually that God may grant us that spirit of compassion which is truly the spirit of God." He says further,

> Even though the poor are often rough and unrefined, we must not judge them from external appearances. On the contrary, if you consider the poor in the light of faith, then you will observe that they are taking the place of the Son of God who chose to be poor.
>
> Since Christ willed to be born poor, He chose for himself disciples who were poor. He

made Himself the servant of the poor and shared their poverty. He went so far as to say that He would consider every deed which either helps or harms the poor as done for or against Himself.

Charity is certainly greater than any rule. Moreover, all rules must lead to charity. With renewed devotion, then, we must serve the poor, especially outcasts and beggars. They have been given to us as our masters and patrons.

Whatever we do for the poor, we do for God. Saint Catherine of Siena tells us, "God said: I have placed you in the midst of your fellows so that you may do to them what you cannot do to Me, and what you do to [them], I count it done to Me." What a great deal for mankind! We should also keep in mind what Saint Thérèse says about charity and actions: "You know well enough that Our Lord does not look so much at the greatness of our actions, nor even at their difficulty, but at the love with which we do them."

While the virtue of charity at times requires that we give up certain things, we must not think that the life of charity is something joyless or anemic. We should be detached from material things, but in a healthy way. Saint Josémaria Escriva (1902-1975) says, "True detachment leads us to be very generous with God and with our fellow men. It makes us actively resourceful and ready to spend ourselves in helping the needy." *The ultimate goal of giving up anything should be more perfect union with God, not detachment for the sake of detachment.*

It should be remembered that charity includes not only giving material support to others in need, but spiritual support as well. For example, praying for someone, or having a Mass said for someone, are acts of charity. It is not necessary to stop the car to get out and lend our help every time we see someone in need. In fact, for some scrupulous people, this course of action would prevent them from ever doing anything else during the day.

In some cases, we may be able to help out directly with material goods (when we have the time and the specific resources someone is looking for); in other cases, we may be able to help out indirectly (by calling the police, for example); in other cases, we may be called to help by simply saying a prayer and moving on with our previous course of action (such as when we see a beggar to whom we have previously offered food or clothing, which was refused in hopes of getting money). The scrupulous should remember the concept of liberty in doubt when it comes to deciding on what type of help to give. Many times we may just be called to say a quick prayer and move on.

We are told by Our Lord to love our neighbor; we are *not* told to love humanity. We should have a general desire to be of help to those who reasonably ask for it, but we are most certainly *not required* to actively help all of humanity at once. We can pray for the whole of humanity, but we cannot actively help more than one person at a time. This should in no way trouble us, but make us relieved that what God asks of us is very reasonable. Indeed, God never commands us to do what is impossible.

Let us remember that charity is the most necessary virtue, the one that lasts with us throughout eternity. Faith enables us to believe all that God has revealed; hope enables us to have a sure expectation of Heaven, yet when we do arrive in Heaven, neither faith nor hope is any longer necessary. Charity alone endures, as we love God above all else and our neighbor as ourselves for the sake of God on earth, as well as in Heaven: "now there remain faith, hope, and charity, these three: but the greatest of these is charity" (1Cor. 13).

Chapter Fourteen:

Developing a Sense of Humor

I need nine hours of sleep a day. The medication I take requires me to eat seven times a day. I like air conditioning and comfortable chairs. I went through all the lives of the saints and I couldn't find one like me.

—Mother Angelica,
Founder of the Eternal Word Television Network (EWTN)

There are some things that are simply not humorous. No matter how we look at them, they are just not funny. Then there are some things that demand serious attention, but not the extreme seriousness that the scrupulous give them. Salvation is a topic that demands such attention, and in fact most people need to take it more seriously. There is no goal more worthy of our attention than that of salvation—our own and that of others.

However, the scrupulous can take salvation so seriously that they actually end up being ridiculous about the matter (see Martin Luther's story in Chapter Three for more on this). Let us not be so obsessed with a goal, that we actually invent requirements regarding the attainment of it; this will only aggravate us and make us less likely to get it.

When we read about saints in order to learn how a good Christian lives, we should of course admire their virtues. However, we should be careful not to assign to them an unreasonable, automated holiness that excludes all possibility of any flaw. Saint Alphonsus speculated, "If the biographers of the saints would write of their defects as well as of their virtues, their biographies would be more voluminous," and he added, "Everyone has defects of character. I have more than others."

The scrupulous can become fixated on the statistics of a saint such as Anthony Mary Claret, and imagine that in order to be a saint, one must be very austere, and never enjoy life. This is not the case, as we will see in the examples of saints who had a well-developed sense of humor. Saint Philip Neri, Saint Thomas More, and Saint Pio of Pietrelcina are all very holy, penitential men, and they all had a great sense of humor. Holiness and humor are not incompatible, and it could be said that not taking *oneself* seriously is actually *required* for holiness.

While we can tell from the quotations of Saint Philip Neri in other parts of this work that he was indeed a truly perceptive man, it may appear from certain actions of his life that he was quite unperceptive, and even crazy. Some people would be shocked to see that a saint would act in such a way. It should be noted, though, that while Saint Philip took the Faith very seriously, he did not take himself too seriously and would not let his penitents do so either. For example, he once had only one side of his beard cut, and went out in public with half a beard; he even directed one of his penitents to do the same. Saint Philip would purposely mispronounce words while reading in public, especially when he knew that people of high education or rank were in attendance. He would also direct some of his penitents, including those of high rank, to beg for alms at the doors of the church.

The goal behind Saint Philip's unusual actions was not merely to amuse himself or others, but to cultivate the virtue of humility. He knew the necessity of humility and sought after it with great zeal. One of the most extraordinary and hilarious penances Saint Philip gave was for a man to lie flat on his face for some time in front of the confessional, in full view of the people nearby. The next time you think your penance is not the right one, think of this penance imposed by Saint Philip, laugh at your pride, be thankful for the penance given to you, and humbly do it.

When we take ourselves too seriously, we become proud and incapable of receiving God's graces. On the other hand, when we laugh at ourselves, we realize how little we are, and open ourselves up so that God can work with us. When we see how small we are in comparison with God, we have a healthier perspective and are able to live out an authentic Christian life based on reality, not on a subjective illusion.

An Austrian psychiatrist thought that Saint Pio of Pietrelcina's stigmata might have had a neurotic origin, so he traveled to Italy to observe the saint. After watching him in good-humored conversation for half an hour, the psychiatrist concluded that the he was not neurotic, because neurotic people, in his words, "have no sense of humor." Saint Pio would tell funny stories during afternoon recreation, including those involving two men from the backwoods. These men had never been on a train before, so when the ticket seller asked them where they wanted to go, one of them replied, "What business is it of yours?"

Once, Saint Pio was sitting with his friend, Joseph Peterson, Pietro Cugino, and a doctor. The saint asked Peterson to do his chicken impression, which he did for the other two men present. Then the doctor asked Saint Pio to do a chicken impression, noting that Joe Peterson was from New York, where they do not have any chickens, and that Saint Pio had been a farm boy. Because of his rural upbringing, one might expect him to do a better chicken impression. The saint then did a weak impression, after which the doctor asked what was wrong with his chicken. Saint Pio replied, "Joseph does a chicken that is well. My chicken is convalescing after paying the doctor bills."

Saint Thomas More had a strong sense of humor as well. He would bring home an animal, such as a monkey, to keep his children amused. Because of his wit and humor, his children even had a tough time knowing if he was serious or only joking with them. In fact, Saint Thomas More was described by one of his friends as being "full of jokes", which he kept telling even up to the point of being executed. It is related that he told his executioners that he might need some help getting up the scaffold for beheading, but as far as getting down, he could manage just fine on his own.

Saint Thérèse apparently even maintained her sense of humor after her death, according to Sister Marie of the Trinity, a close companion of Saint Thérèse at the Carmelite monastery in Lisieux. According to custom, the body of a deceased nun was put in a coffin near the grill separating the nuns from the visiting laity. This way, the laity could view the deceased, and pass rosaries through the grill to a nun standing by, who would touch them to the body of the deceased and return them to the laity.

The body of Saint Thérèse was put out in this way for viewing, with the laity passing their rosaries through the grill. When Sister Marie was on duty near the grill, she could not stop crying, due to her sadness at the passing of such a dear friend. When one visitor handed Sister Marie a rosary to be touched to the remains of Saint Thérèse and passed back, something very odd happened: the rosary would not get loose from the hands of Saint Thérèse.

Amidst her tears and attempts to get the rosary loose, Sister Marie thought she heard Saint Thérèse saying to her interiorly, "I'm not going to let go until you give me a smile." Sister Marie replied, interiorly, "No, I feel like crying; I'm not going to smile." The visitor then questioned Sister Marie about why it was taking so long for her to get the rosary back. Sister Marie realized how amusing the whole thing was, and finally laughed. After this, Saint Thérèse seemed to let go of the rosary, as it was untangled.

What exactly is a sense of humor anyway? It is taking amusement in seeing that things are not as they ought to be. Scrupulous souls are half-way to having a great sense of humor, as they tend to see what is wrong with everything. In other words, the scrupulous are very skilled, even overly-skilled, at seeing that certain things are not what they *ought to be*. In fact, if something is ninety-five percent correct, the scrupulous tend to focus on the five percent that is incorrect, to the exclusion of all that is right. This lack of proper focus, along with an absence of amusement, tends to produce much anxiety and confusion in the mind, and is an obstacle to receiving God's graces.

However, when the scrupulous take amusement at the incongruity between what is and what should be, they have a sense of humor. It is true that some things are simply not funny, but the scrupulous should expand their horizons in this regard, especially when it comes to oneself. If you cannot laugh at yourself, everyone else will.

In the spirit of taking oneself more lightly, the following list has been formulated. If any of these five items describe you, then you are likely scrupulous, and should probably take yourself less seriously:

> 1) One of your most commonly uttered phrases is, "I know I asked this already, but..."
> 2) You have actually thought your hands were dirtier *after* you had washed them.
> 3) You think that anything worth doing once is worth doing twice—per minute.
> 4) You think buying Quaker Oats constitutes an act of apostasy.
> 5) You are not sure if you just read this list or not.

Saint Teresa of Avila stated, "A sad nun is a bad nun. I am more afraid of one unhappy sister than a crowd of evil spirits. What would happen if we hid what little sense of humor we had? Let each of us humbly use this to cheer others." This is true not only of nuns, but of all of us. We conclude this chapter with more wise words of Saint Teresa of Avila: "From somber, serious, sullen saints, save us, O Lord."

Chapter Fifteen:

Selecting and Obeying Your Spiritual Director

There is nothing which gives greater security to our actions, or more effectively cuts the snares the devil lays for us, than to follow another person's will, rather than our own, in doing good.

—Saint Philip Neri

It tends to be easy to view someone else's life objectively, but very difficult to see our own lives in the same way. There are all kinds of subjective challenges that prevent us from seeing things accurately, such as fears, misconceptions, hurts, and our own pride. All these things distort in our mind what is clear to everyone else, cloud our reasoning, and make sound decisions very difficult, if not impossible, to come by.

A question posed from a friend may be answered immediately, yet the very same question, when it applies to one's own life, may take months to answer! We simply do not see others and ourselves in the same light. Everyone else's problems are simple to get around, yet ours are just too troubling—or so it seems.

For example, a scrupulous Mr. Smith may wonder about whether a lie he told was a mortal sin. It happened when someone caught him off guard and asked him an unexpected question. He barely had time to think and quickly lied, as it seemed to be the only way out of the situation. Mr. Smith asks a friend, Mr. Jones, what he thinks, and this friend analyzes the facts: Mr. Smith did not have the time for full knowledge and full consent. Thus, two of the three conditions for a mortal sin are not met, so even if the issue were over grave matter, it still would not be a mortal sin. Furthermore, Mr. Smith's lie may not have been a sin at all, as there was almost no time for him to think and act with deliberation, and only deliberate acts of the will can be sins.

Mr. Jones explains that while it is often said that sin is any thought, word, or deed contrary to the will of God, this definition is missing something critical: *deliberation*. Sin is any *deliberate* thought, word, or deed contrary to the will of God. Where there is no deliberation, there is no sin, just as where there is no deliberation, there is no virtue. Acts that are not under the control of our will are not rewarded or punished. (Thus, it is not possible to sin or to do anything virtuous while sleeping.) Because of lack of premeditation on the part of Mr. Smith, Mr. Jones informs him that the lie he told was not a mortal sin.

The curious thing about this story is that if the roles were reversed, the scrupulous Mr. Smith would likely be able to tell Mr. Jones that his un-premeditated lie is not a mortal sin, and tell him this quickly. The same question, applied to someone else's life, is easy for us to answer, even when we ourselves are scrupulous. It is so much easier for us to see others accurately and give sound advice to them than it is for us to see ourselves accurately, and make sound decisions.

The saints knew this, and sought out an objective view of their lives from someone else: a spiritual director. Saint Bernard of Clairvaux asserts, "Whoever constitutes himself his own master, becomes the disciple of a fool." Indeed, we end up being fools when we follow our own will, rather than that of another, doing good. Saint Vincent de Paul tells us,

> The first step to be taken by one who wishes to follow Christ is, according to Our Lord's words, that of renouncing himself—that is, his own senses, his own passions, his own will, his own judgment, making to God a sacrifice of all these things which are surely sacrifices very acceptable to the Lord.

Interestingly, it is easy to fall prey to self-deception when it comes to renouncing self. We can flatter ourselves that we are very mortified, humble, and selfless, when in fact what we have is a very refined selfishness. This calls for a practical step in overcoming the problem, and the most practical way of renouncing self is to be held responsible to a spiritual director. It goes without saying that the director should be orthodox, but he should also be patient, compassionate, and decisive. It is true that such a combination can be difficult to find in one person, but there are great priests out there that fit this description well.

It may be objected by someone who frequents several confessors, that he already has a spiritual director. This is quite true: his spiritual director is himself. He goes from confessor to confessor gathering advice, some of which he uses, most of which he does not. He goes in search not of God's Will, but his own. The result of this course of action is not peace of mind, but more confusion. Saint Vincent de Paul says, "When someone places confidence in his own prudence, knowledge, and intelligence, God, to make him know and see his insufficiency, withdraws from him His help and leaves him to work by himself."

Let us not be foolish by trusting in our own knowledge and judgment; let us be wise by trusting in the judgment of a minister of God. This is the way to peace of mind: active faith in God that He will safely guide us through His minister, whom we obey for the sake of God.

Preparing to select and obey a spiritual director can be a difficult step for a scrupulous soul, yet it is an essential step to be taken in becoming better. Often times the very things that terrify us the most are those that end up helping us the most. What is needed is prayerful trust in God's truth, providence and mercy. Ask God which priest He wants to act as His representative in your life, whom you should obey as your director.

Saint Philip Neri tells us, "Before a man chooses his confessor, he ought to think well about it, and pray about it also; but once he has chosen, he ought not to change, except for the most urgent reasons, but put the utmost confidence in his director." He further states, "Those who are desirous of progressing in the way of God should submit themselves to a prudent confessor, whom they should obey in God's place. By so doing, we are certain of not having to render an account to God of (our) actions." Saint Alphonsus is in complete agreement, saying: "Let those who wish to make progress in the ways of God choose for themselves a competent spiritual director whom they should obey as they would God Himself."

The one thing above all others that will bring peace of mind is obedience to one's director. Obedience is an act of humility, while disobedience is an act of pride. To put oneself above a minister of God is not at all what God wants from us. He wants us rather to obey those who have been ordained His ministers and pastors of the Church. Our Lord tells His ministers, "He that heareth you heareth me: and he that despiseth you despiseth me: and he that despiseth me despiseth him that sent me" (Lk. 10:16). In light of this, it easy to see how Saint Philip can say, "He who always acts under obedience, may rest assured that he will not have to give an account of his actions to God."

Some people may see spiritual direction as somehow limiting their freedom, which is not at all the goal. The main goal of spiritual direction is to free one up to live virtuously—-to free him from himself, the world, and the devil, in order to live out God's Will effectively. He who sins becomes a slave to sin, and he who practices virtue, becomes more and more free to practice it. This is the goal of spiritual direction: the perfect freedom of holy virtue.

If one is in doubt about whether he should follow the advice of his confessor, it is certain that he should. It is only when one is *certain* about the sinfulness of an action that he must not do it. Remember, where there is doubt, there is freedom, and you are free to do what your confessor tells you. If he gives you a penance of saying one Our Father, and you think the penance should be an entire rosary, do not be troubled. Say the one Our Father. The one Our Father is sufficient to fulfill the penance, because it is the one that your director gave you.

It is also true that the penances specifically given by a confessor have special merit in God's eyes, even though materially they may be lesser than others we could think up or desire to do on our own. Therefore, let us humbly accept them and submit to the wisdom of God, which ordains that we follow the judgment of His ministers and not our own.

Saint Alphonsus, himself a Doctor of the Church, says, "The principle of obeying one's spiritual director in all doubts of conscience is confirmed unanimously by all the Doctors of the Church." He also states,

> Scrupulous souls should realize that not only is the path of obedience the secure way for them, but that they are obliged to obey their spiritual directors and at the same time to disregard their scruples and to act quite freely in all their doubts.

Saint Philip Neri agrees, saying, "The scrupulous should submit themselves always and in everything to the judgment of their confessor, and accustom themselves to have a contempt for their own scruples."

To see how valuable obedience is in the sight of God, let us hear a story from Saint Alphonsus:

> The Venerable Catherine of Cardona, having left the Spanish Court, retired into a desert, where she lived for many years in the practice of penitential austerities, the very recital of which would fill the mind with horror. In her life it is related that seeing one day a Discalced Carmelite carrying, through obedience, a bundle of wood, and knowing by inspiration that he murmured interiorly against the command of his superior, she thus addressed him: 'Brother, carry with readiness those sticks and be assured that by this act of obedience you will merit a greater reward than I have deserved by all my penances.'

Obedience in small things is more valuable to God than doing great penances according our own will. The interior disposition of the penitent is far more important than the outward material action. In this light, Saint Alphonsus reminds us,

> By your obedience you will merit a greater reward and will make greater progress in virtue than you would by many spontaneous acts of penance and devotion. A great servant of God used to say that to perform a single act of abnegation of self-will is more profitable than to build a thousand hospitals.

He goes on to ask,

> From what source arise all our troubles? Do they not spring from attachment to our own inclinations? 'From what source' says Saint Bernard, 'is disturbance of mind, if not from following self-will?' Attachment to self-will is the only reason why so many religious lead an unhappy life. How can [a nun] expect to enjoy peace when, instead of practicing obedience, she obliges her superiors to submit to her desires?

Saint Alphonsus had in mind women religious specifically, but is it not obvious that what he says applies to all of us, whether men, women, religious, priests, or laity? Saint Philip Neri informs us, "When the devil has failed in making a man fall, he puts forward all his energies to create distrust between the penitent and the confessor, and so by little and little he gains his end at last." Let us not fall prey to the lies of the devil, who wants to drive a wedge between penitent and director. Instead, let us trust in God, whose minister we obey for His sake.

Saint Ignatius of Loyola says, "If you have true humility and submissiveness, your scruples will not cause you so much trouble. Pride is the fuel they feed on, and it is pride that places more reliance on one's own judgment and less on the judgment of others whom we trust." In Proverbs 3:5–6 we are exhorted to "Have confidence in the Lord with all thy heart, and lean not upon thy own prudence [understanding]. In all thy ways think on him: and he will direct thy steps."

True security does not come from second-guessing or overruling our director, but from obeying him. Let us free ourselves by giving over our responsibility into the hands of God's minister, and be at peace with his directions. Let us follow the advice of Saint Francis de Sales when he instructs us as follows:

> This is the one piece of advice above all others; no matter how long you search or where you search, you will never find a more secure way of ascertaining the will of God than the way of humble submission to one's spiritual director. This is the way recommended and practiced by all the saints.

What more do we need to hear? Along with the enlightenment from the saints on the matter, all we need to do is pray for the strength to carry it out, and then do so.

Chapter Sixteen:

Receiving Our Lord in Holy Communion

You are not approaching Holy Communion because you are endeavoring to sanctify the Lord; He it is who is to sanctify you.
—Saint Bonaventure

Attending the Holy Sacrifice of the Mass is an awesome privilege—how blessed we are to be in a position to receive all the graces that Our Lord won for us by His sacrifice on Calvary! The Mass is an ocean of graces from start to finish, graces which cannot be exhausted in this life. If Our Lord promised to reward the giving of a cup of cold water in His name, how much more rewarding is attending Mass, where we are able to offer God the Son to the God the Father as the perfect sacrifice for our sins!

It is true that he who attends Mass without receiving Holy Communion is far better off than he who does not attend at all, and it is also true that we are not required to receive Holy Communion except once a year. However, in addition to the many graces offered to us throughout the Mass, Our Lord allows us to partake of His body, blood, soul, and divinity in Holy Communion.

God can never be outdone in benevolence, so instead of standing back and letting us fall on our own; He descends to our level and makes our sanctification simple for us. God takes the initiative, but it is up to us to accept His invitation into the divine life of the Most Holy Trinity. This is the grace of Holy Communion: the gift of sanctifying grace—literally the life of the soul—the most important gift God has for us.

In short, God wants us to be partakers of the divine nature. Saint Pio of Pietrelcina says, "In the most Holy Sacrament of the Eucharist, in this sacrament of love, we have true life and true happiness. In it we receive not only those graces that perfect us, but the very author of those graces."

Our Lord, who is that "very author," tells us in the Gospel of John, Chapter Six, that

> He that eats my flesh, and drinks my blood, has everlasting life: and I will raise him up in the last day. For my flesh is meat indeed: and my blood is drink indeed. He that eats my flesh and drinks my blood abides in me, and I in him. As the living Father hath sent me, and I live by the Father; so he that eats me, the same also shall live by me. This is the bread that came down from heaven. Not as your fathers did eat manna, and are dead. He that eats this bread shall live forever.

Saint John Vianney adds that if you compare "all the good works in the world" with one reception of Holy Communion, all the good works "will be like a grain of dust beside a mountain." Stop and think about that: you could spend your entire life doing works of penance, the likes of which the world has never before witnessed, yet in receiving Our Lord once in Holy Communion, you have done something incomparably more pleasing to Him than all those other works put together. Why is this? Because, as Saint Pio said, when we receive Holy Communion, we not only receive graces, but the ultimate source of those graces: Our Lord Himself. It is not possible to be closer to Our Lord while on earth than when we receive Him in Holy Communion.

It should be expected for a Catholic to be profoundly reverent at Mass, and most especially so when receiving Holy Communion. However, there is a difference between profound reverence and holding oneself up to an impossible standard. Scrupulous souls tend to fret over being "worthy" to receive Holy Communion. It is true that the expression "worthy reception of Holy Communion" is commonly used. However, while this expression is common, it is not accurate.

Strictly speaking, there is no worthiness at all between God and us—there is an infinite distance in dignity. This distance cannot be bridged, except in a certain sense, when we receive Holy Communion. Saint Catherine of Siena says to the scrupulous, "Of course you are unworthy. But when do you hope to be worthy? All the good works that we could ever do would never make us worthy of Holy Communion. God alone is worthy of Himself, He alone can make us worthy of Him."

Only a God would be worthy of receiving a God, so let us not be ridiculous enough to hold ourselves to such an impossible standard of holiness. Let us instead humbly recognize our weakness and get the strength we need from receiving Holy Communion. Saint Ignatius of Loyola tells us,

> One of the most admirable effects of Holy
> Communion is to preserve souls from falling,
> and to help those who fall from weakness to rise
> again. Therefore, it is much more profitable to
> approach the Divine Sacrament frequently, with
> love, respect, and confidence, than to keep back
> from an excess of fear.

It is unfortunately true that many people do not appreciate the great gift of Holy Communion. Many people go to Mass once or twice a year, if they go at all. Others go more often but receive Our Lord carelessly by talking to their neighbor instead of praying before Holy Communion, and then running out of church before Mass is over. This is a sad reality, but is it not all the more reason for those of us who do revere the Lord to receive Him devoutly in Holy Communion?

Your reverence will be a good example to others: with hands folded in prayer, focusing on Our Lord's great love as you walk up the aisle to the Communion rail, asking Mary and Joseph to receive Jesus for you, as you cannot do it as humbly as they did, and then reverently receive Our Lord on the tongue. Slowly returning to the pew and thanking God on your knees, you then ask for the graces you need most. This is the time when we are closest to Our Lord, when we are made to share in His divine life. As Mary received Our Lord at the Incarnation, so do we receive Him in Holy Communion. What an awesome privilege we should take advantage of!

Before receiving Holy Communion, Satan may attempt to scare us into staying in the pew. All kinds of irrelevant fears may be presented: someone might take your seat while you are gone, everyone is looking at you, food might be stuck to your teeth, and on and on. Do not be surprised when these silly ideas occur—

there is no limit to the number or intensity of vain fears that could be presented to you, as Satan is absolutely shameless. Be at peace then, and hold the silly ideas in contempt, not giving them any power over you.

While we cannot control all the thoughts that come to our minds, we can control what we do, despite any thoughts that may occur. One of the great things you will find is that when you consistently act with confidence and trust in God, despite vain fears, these fears will become weaker and less frequent. You are essentially starving them to death, and instead are feeding the faithful thoughts, which will grow stronger.

Saint Faustina Kowalska (1905–1938) struggled with fears of receiving Holy Communion, and describes her victory over them thus,

> When it seemed to me that I should not communicate [that is, receive Our Lord in Holy Communion], I went, before Holy Communion, to the Directress and told her that I could not approach the sacrament because it seemed to me that I should not do so. But she would not permit me to omit Holy Communion, so I went, and I understand now that it was only obedience that saved me.
>
> The Directress told me later that my trial has passed quickly, 'and this solely because you were obedient, Sister, and it was though the power of obedience that you struggled through this so bravely.'

Even the most severe priest this author ever met stated that when in doubt about whether or not to receive Holy Communion, one should go up and do so. Can there be any more reasonable discussion about the matter? Our Lord wants us to receive Him into our body and soul, in order to become inseparably united with Him in this Most Holy Sacrament. Let us not give in to unreasonable fears, but wholeheartedly accept Our Lord's invitation to live in His divine love.

One more note on reception of Holy Communion: the scrupulous can be concerned about particles of the host falling to the ground or otherwise being ill-treated. This concern is a very good thing in itself, and certainly every Catholic should share in it. However, just like all good things, it can be overdone. We can get so caught up in fear of irreverence of the Holy Eucharist that we see this irreverence even where it does not occur. If you are looking for something, you will likely find it, even if it is not there.

One rule that will eliminate much of the excessive concern about Eucharistic particles is to receive Holy Communion only on the tongue. This is the traditional manner of reception, and is still the norm for the Church as a whole. Reception in the hand is only an indult, and carries with it many problems, one of which is the risk of particles falling to the ground. Reception on the tongue is the safest and most reverent way to receive Our Lord.

A second rule that will eliminate much of the excessive concern about Eucharistic particles is to realize that it is primarily the responsibility of the priest (and, if present, the altar server holding a paten) that no particles fall to the ground. The priest is in a far better position to see if such a thing occurs than the communicant is. You may wish to talk with your pastor about your concern, and ask him to take a load off of your mind by assuring you that he will certainly make sure that no particles fall to the ground, and that you are not responsible in this matter.

Saint Thérèse tells us, "Our Lord does not come down from Heaven every day to lie in a golden ciborium. He comes to find another heaven which is infinitely dearer to him—the heaven of our souls, created in His image, the living temples of the Adorable Trinity." Let us be at peace then, and take to heart what Saint Pio wrote to one of his penitents: "Remember what I have told you so often: as long as we are not certain of being in serious sin, we need not abstain from [Holy] Communion."

Chapter Seventeen:

Sacramentals

Sacramentals are sacred signs that signify spiritual effects that are obtained though the prayers of the Church. Unlike the sacraments, sacramentals were not instituted directly by Our Lord, but by His Church. While they are inferior to the sacraments, they do prepare us in special ways to receive graces through the sacraments. It is very beneficial to learn about and use sacramentals, because the person who does so receives more grace than the one who does not.

There are numerous sacramentals, all of which cannot be covered here. However, four of the best-known and most-used ones will be explained briefly.

HOLY WATER

When we use holy water, we renew our baptismal promises of rejecting sin and accepting Jesus Christ. Holy water has great power over evil spirits and helps to bring about peace of mind. Saint Teresa of Avila experienced this power in her own life, and explains it here:

> I was once in the oratory. [The devil] appeared to me in an] abominable form at my left side. He told me in a terrifying way that I had really freed myself from his hands but that he would

catch me with them again. I was struck with great fear and blessed myself as best I could; he disappeared, but returned right away. I didn't know what to do. There was some holy water there, and I threw it in that direction; he never returned again.

I often experience that there is nothing the devils flee from more—without returning— than holy water. They also flee from the cross, but they return. The power of holy water must be great. For me there is a particular and very noticeable consolation my soul experiences upon taking it. Without a doubt my soul feels ordinarily a refreshment I would not know how to explain, like an interior delight that comforts it entirely. This is something that has happened often and that I have observed carefully. Let us say the relief is like that coming to a person, very hot and thirsty, when he drinks a jar of cold water; it would seem that he felt the refreshment all over.

I consider everything ordained by the Church to be important, and I rejoice to see the power of those words [of blessing by the priest] recited over the water so that its difference from unblessed water becomes so great.

Let us be sure to keep a great supply of holy water with us. We should have at least two separate containers of it in the house at all times, so that if one container runs out, we immediately have a new one to use. Let us be bold with the amount we have, not relying on those tiny holy water containers, but getting large containers that are not even made specifically for holy water. Keeping smaller amounts with us in the car, or on our person, is helpful as well.

Brown Scapular

A scapular is most commonly known as two small, square pieces of cloth connected by cords, and usually worn over the shoulders. These small scapulars are derived from the larger scapulars of various religious orders, and they represent devotion to a specific kind of spirituality (Franciscan, Dominican, etc).

The most well-known scapular is the Brown Scapular of Our Lady of Mount Carmel, which is taken from the scapular of the Carmelite Order and is a sign of consecration to Our Lady of Mount Carmel. Those who wear it have a special devotion to Our Lady, which is usually manifested in daily recitation of the rosary.

Those who wear the Brown Scapular entrust their salvation to Jesus through Mary, who promises us, "Those who die wearing this scapular shall not suffer eternal fire." Heaven will be the final home of those who wear the Brown Scapular with devotion to Our Lady. The reason for this is not that the two pieces of cloth have any special power, but that Our Lady's intercession, our earnest devotion to her and her son, and the blessing of the scapular, all combine into an unconquerable force working toward final perseverance and therefore, sainthood.

Once a priest blesses the scapular, the person should wear it as a sign of his devotion to Jesus though Mary. The scapular blessing attaches to each new scapular the person may use in subsequent years. After enrollment through the blessing of the priest, one may use a scapular medal instead of the cloth scapular, but unlike the cloth scapular, each subsequent scapular medal a person may use must be blessed.

Rosary

Saint Louis de Montfort says, "The rosary is a blessed blending of mental and vocal prayer by which we honor and learn to imitate the mysteries and virtues of the life, death, passion, and glory of Jesus and Mary." In other words, the rosary is the prayer of the Gospel. Saint Louis continues:

> Since the Holy Rosary is composed, principally and in substance, of the Prayer of Christ and the Angelic Salutation, that is, the Our Father and the Hail Mary, it was without doubt the first prayer and the first devotion of the faithful, and has been in use all through the centuries from the time of the Apostles and disciples down to the present.
>
> It was only in the year 1214, however, that Holy Mother Church received the Rosary in its present form and according to the method we use today. It was given to the Church by Saint Dominic (1170-1221) who had received it from the Blessed Virgin as a powerful means of converting the Albigensians and other sinners.

Many sinners of modern times can give credit for their conversion to praying the rosary, such as Blessed Bartolo Longo (see Chapter Four). The rosary has lost none of its power, and we are blessed to be able to pray it today.

Among Our Lady's fifteen promises to those who pray the rosary are:

> Two: I promise my special protection and the greatest graces to all those who shall recite the Rosary.

Four: The Rosary will cause virtue and good works to flourish; it will obtain for souls the abundant mercy of God; it will withdraw the hearts of men from the love of the world and its vanities, and will lift them to the desire for eternal things. Oh, that souls would sanctify themselves by this means.

Eight: Those who are faithful to recite the Rosary shall have during their life and at their death the light of God and the plenitude of His graces; at the moment of death they shall participate in the merits of the saints in paradise.

Fourteen: All who recite the Rosary are my sons and daughters, and brothers and sisters of my only son Jesus Christ.

Pope Pius XII says, "There is no surer means of calling down God's blessings upon the family than the daily recitation of the rosary." Let us take Our Lady's promises and the advice of the Holy Father to heart, and pray the rosary daily. What a great way to unite ourselves with the Gospel message and thereby receive God's graces.

Remember that when one is in doubt about whether he completed a prayer or set of prayers, he can presume he has, and need not repeat them. For example, when one is unsure if he completed a decade of the rosary, he can presume he has done so, even if he is unsure a single prayer of it was prayed. When in doubt, he may presume completion and move on to the next decade.

MIRACULOUS MEDAL

The Medal of the Immaculate Conception, or as it is more commonly known, the Miraculous Medal, was designed by the Blessed Virgin Mary and given to Saint Catherine Labouré (1806-1876) in France in 1830. Through a series of apparitions, Our Lady showed Saint Catherine what the medals would look like, and instructed her to have them made. Those who would wear the medal would receive great graces, Saint Catherine was told.

In the apparitions, Our Lady was standing on a globe with a serpent crushed beneath her feet, reminiscent of Genesis 3:15. She was holding another globe in her hand, which represented the entire world, but most especially France, which at the time was experiencing many difficulties. Rays of light, symbolizing the graces Mary obtains for those who ask her, streamed from her fingers. Around this scene were the words, "O Mary, conceived without sin, pray for us who have recourse to thee."

It was also revealed to Saint Catherine what the back of the medal would look like. A large "M", out of which a cross appeared, was surrounded by twelve stars, which represent the twelve Apostles, and in another way, the Church in general. Beneath this were the Sacred Heart of Jesus and the Immaculate Heart of Mary—the one crowned with thorns, the other pierced by a sword. Both sides of the medal call to mind what Saint John wrote in the Apocalypse, 12:1, "A great sign appeared in heaven: a woman clothed with the sun, and the moon was under her feet, and upon her head a crown of twelve stars."

Our Lady told Saint Catherine, "Have a medal struck upon this model. Those who wear it will receive great graces, especially if they wear it around the neck." Saint Catherine described the apparitions to her confessor, with whom she worked to have the medals made. The first medals were made in 1832 and Mary's promise was shown to be true, through the many blessings received by those who wore the medal.

Chapter Eighteen:
Natural Remedies

In this book we have dealt primarily with the supernatural aspects of scrupulosity, such as grace, prayer, and the sacraments. However, we are not disembodied spirits, but a wondrous combination of soul and body. While the soul is more important than the body, this is not at all to say that the body has no meaning. We pray and receive the sacraments with our bodies, and are saved by the sacrifice of Our Lord's body and blood. It is in this light that some natural aspects of scrupulosity will be touched upon here.

Moderation is a key issue for the scrupulous in spiritual concerns, and also in natural ones. One extreme is to be careless about our health, and the other extreme is to care too much about our health. Saint Alphonsus states,

> A discreet attention to the preservation of health, with a view to be better able to serve God, is not a defect, but an act of virtue. But a superfluous

> solicitude about health is a fault; and aided by
> self-love, makes many unnecessary indulgences
> appear indispensable.

There are stories about certain saints (such as Saint Anthony Mary Claret in Chapter Fourteen) who practiced severe penances, such as eating or sleeping very little, and/or working very much. This is something to be admired, but not necessarily imitated, because God does not call us to aim for statistics, but for the virtue of charity. It is the rare person who is even capable of doing extraordinary penances, let alone called to do them.

Many people would be surprised to read the following words from Saint Peter of Alcantara (1499–1562), who himself was known for great penances: "One should never deny the body what is due to it, that the body itself may not hinder what is due to the soul." It is possible for someone to practice such severe penances that he actually makes himself incapable of performing his ordinary duties in life. Needless to say, this defeats the very purpose any penance is for. We are not called to torture ourselves in a desperate attempt to "keep up with the Joneses" spiritually.

For example, a misguided soul may become so obsessed with a "fast" from sleep that he weakens himself to the point of being unable to attend Sunday Mass. In such a case, the soul focuses on his strange ideas about mortification to the detriment of his own true good. Sleep deprivation is not required of us, but attendance at Sunday Mass is. Saint Alphonsus says that spiritual directors should be loath to give permission for mortification in the area of sleep, since this can often be harmful both to soul and body. Without sufficient sleep, one is easily confused and probably unable to meditate, and is in no form for other acts of devotion.

Saint John Vianney agrees, stating,

> Religion is sometimes misunderstood. For instance, my children, here is a person who has to do a day's work. She has an idea of performing great penances, to spend the night in prayer; if she is well instructed she will say to herself: 'No, I must not do these things or I shall not be fit to do my duty tomorrow. I shall be sleepy, and the least thing will make me irritable; I shall be cross all day; I shall not do half the work I should have done had I [taken] my night's rest.' A well instructed person always has two guides: counsel and obedience.

We should exercise due diligence in trying to get things done, yet as human beings, we also need to relax regularly, otherwise we will overload and exhaust ourselves. Saint Francis de Sales says, "It is a failing to be so harsh and rigid that we will not allow ourselves or others to indulge in any recreation." We all need a break from work to enjoy a garden, a game, grandchildren, etc., or simply to rest. If we do not give ourselves adequate rest, we will find that our bodies will force us into resting when we would rather be engaging in work.

A cause or contributing factor to scruples can be natural—such as lack of sleep, poor nutrition, or overwork. The same person can have two entirely different outlooks on life, depending on his physical health. He may be a pleasant, optimistic fellow when he has gotten sufficient amount of sleep, but cranky pessimist when he has not gotten enough. The same is true with food and work—the right amount of both is needed in order to have a good mindset. Too much or too little of something will leave us unbalanced physically and spiritually.

In one circumstance the scrupulous may think clearly and make good decisions, while in another, they may have confused thoughts and become seemingly incapable of making a good decision. This is where being physically healthy comes into play. We should, as far as is reasonably possible, be healthy individuals. It is not a luxury to get enough sleep. It is not a luxury to eat enough food. It is not a luxury to have a balanced work schedule. All of these things are simply a part of being a healthy individual. Being under-rested, under-fed, and over-worked may cause scruples, or make dealing with scruples that much more difficult.

Now, here are a few types of foods that can be helpful, and some to be avoided. Bananas can be helpful for the scrupulous, in part because they contain serotonin, which helps to regulate one's mood. Turkey can also be helpful, because it contains a precursor of serotonin. Calcium and vitamin D can also be helpful in calming one down. One should make sure to get enough protein, because lack of protein makes one light-headed.

Caffeine and foods high in simple carbohydrates (sugar) should be avoided. This does not mean, however, that one must stop eating all simple carbohydrates. Also, complex carbohydrates do not cause the trouble that large amounts of simple carbohydrates do, because they provide a more steady flow of energy, rather than a sudden spike in energy.

Hand washing can be a great trouble to the scrupulous. When it is possible, it can be very helpful to delay hand washing for five minutes, or another allotted amount of time. For example, if someone takes out the garbage and then feels an urgent need to wash his hands, simply sitting down and peacefully waiting for five minutes will help (even if no prayer is involved, although, as we have seen earlier in this book, prayer helps even more). At the end of the five minutes, he can wash his hands more effectively, getting the dirt off using less water and less soap. Why is this so? Simply because he has "let the storm pass" so to speak, and is better able to take in the reality before him, rather than a fear-inspired perception of what is not really there. Something intensely feared has a tendency to present itself, even its very absence.

In general, we can take to heart the words of Father Alfred Wilson, who says of phobias, "The more ruthlessly they are trampled on the better. Phobias are bullies; give in to them and they become paralyzing tyrants. Combat them and they soon slink off like miserable cowards."

Conclusion

Saint Alphonsus says, "Scruples are [like] a species of pitch that, the more it is handled, the more it adheres; the more you reflect on [the scruples], the more you fill your mind with darkness." The first tendency of the scrupulous soul is to think his way out of a problem, yet this only brings about more problems. The answer then, is to pray (as opposed to merely thinking), to recognize and live the concept of liberty in doubt, and to obey one's director in all that is not certainly sinful.

We should also realize that our intention is far more important than our material actions, or the results of those actions. What counts is not accomplishing things with extreme exactitude, but taking the necessary time to learn what should be done in a given situation and then simply doing what should be done. Even if, through no fault of our own, we do something from a good motive that is (unknown to us) materially wrong, there is no formal sin involved. Sin is deliberately going against God's will; where there is no evil deliberation, there is no sin.

We must remember that God's Providence extends to all times, all places, and all people. There is nothing in the world that happens which God is not aware of, nothing that takes Him by surprise, even the most heinous sins. This is not to say that God supports sin, but that God is almighty and therefore can make good come out of evil. We see the prime example of this in the sacrifice of the Son of God on the Cross of Calvary, which is the cause of our redemption.

Saint Philip Neri reminds us, "We must always remember that God does everything well, although we may not see the reason of what He does." Saint Catherine of Siena expands on this, saying, "Everything comes from love. All is ordained for the salvation of man. God does nothing without this goal in mind."

Our omnipotent God is infinitely happy in Himself, in no need of anyone or anything else, yet He created us out of nothing so that we could love Him. He goes so far as to reduce Himself to appearing as mere bread. How is it possible that anyone could disbelieve in God's love for us when He has humbled Himself so much? If a human being were able to reduce himself to appear as bread for the love of us, this would indeed be quite remarkable. Yet we have not a human being, but the eternal and almighty God doing just this! He comes down from Heaven every day in the Mass out of His infinite love for us.

We conclude with yet another fitting quote from our patron, Saint Alphonsus Liguori:

> Scrupulous souls should accept the sufferings which their scrupulosity causes in a spirit of resignation; they should not forget in the midst of their trials that God permits these for their benefit, that they might grow in humility, that they might be more careful in avoiding certainly

gravely dangerous occasions of sin, that they might more frequently recommend themselves to the Lord, and that they might have greater trust in the divine goodness.

They should have frequent recourse to the Mother of God, who is called Mother of Mercy and Comforter of the Afflicted. They should be convinced that by obeying blindly their spiritual director they will never be abandoned by the Lord, Who wishes all to be saved and will never allow a truly obedient soul to be lost...

'The Lord is my light and my salvation, whom should I fear?' (Ps. 26:1).

Helpful Prayers

Here are some prayers that are helpful for the scrupulous. It is *not* necessary to memorize them immediately and say them all every day. The purpose of any prayer is to further one's progress toward a fuller union with God, not to hinder such progress; so taking one prayer at a time is a good rule to follow.

PRAYER FOR SIMPLICITY
Jesus, help me to simplify my life by learning what you want me to be—and becoming that person.

—Saint Thérèse

PRAYER FOR DIVINE MERCY
Eternal Father, for the sake of Our Lord's sorrowful passion, have mercy on us and on the whole world.

ACT OF CONFIDENCE IN GOD
Lord, without your help I can do nothing; with your help I can do all things, though Christ Who strengthens me.

SHORT VERSION OF THE LITANY OF HUMILITY

O Jesus meek and humble of heart,

Hear me.

From the desire of being honored,
Deliver me, O Jesus.

From the desire of being praised,
Deliver me, O Jesus.

From the fear of being ridiculed,
Deliver me, O Jesus.

From the fear of being humiliated,
Deliver me, O Jesus.

That others may be esteemed more than I,
Jesus, grant me the grace to desire it.

That others may become holier than I, provided I become as holy as I should.

Jesus, grant me the grace to desire it.

—Cardinal Merry del Val (1865-1930),
Secretary of State for Pope Saint Pius X

VENI SANCTE SPIRITUS

Come Holy Ghost, fill the hearts of Thy faithful and enkindle in them the fire of Thy love. Send forth Thy spirit and they shall be created and Thou shall renew the face of the earth. Let us pray. O God, who by the light of the Holy Spirit didst instruct the hearts of thy faithful, grant that by the gifts of same spirit we may be always truly wise and ever rejoice in His consolations, through Christ our Lord. Amen.

ANIMA CHRISTI
Soul of Christ, be my sanctification,
Body of Christ, be my salvation,
Blood of Christ, fill all my veins,
Water from the side of Christ, wash out my stains,
Passion of Christ, my comfort be,
Oh good Jesus, listen to me.
Within Thy wounds I fain would hide,
Never to be parted from Thy side.
Guard me when the foe assails me,
Call me when my life shall fail me,
Bid me come to Thee above,
With Thy saints to sing Thy love,
World without end. Amen.

PRAYER OF GUIDANCE
Grant me, I beseech thee, O merciful God, ardently to desire, prudently to study, rightly to understand, and perfectly to fulfill, that which is pleasing to thee, to the praise and glory of Thy name. Amen.

—Saint Thomas Aquinas

ACT OF CONFIDENCE IN THE MOTHER OF GOD
Having confidence in you, O Mother of God, I shall be saved. Being under your protection, I shall fear nothing. With your help I shall give battle to my enemies and put them to flight; for devotion to you is an arm of salvation.

—Saint John Damascene (676–749)

CONSECRATION TO MARY
To thee I commit all my anxieties and sorrows, my life and the end of my life, that by thy most holy intercession, and by thy merits, all my actions may be directed and governed by thy will and that of thy Son.

—Saint Aloysius Gonzaga (1568–1591)

CONSECRATION TO MARY

I am all yours, and all that I have belongs to you, O Jesus, through Mary, your holy Mother.

—Saint Louis de Montfort

PRAYER TO SAINT JOSEPH

O Glorious Saint Joseph, spouse of the Immaculate Virgin, obtain for me a pure, humble, and charitable mind and perfect resignation to the divine will. Be my guide, father, and model through life, so that I may merit to die as thou didst die, in the arms of Jesus and Mary. Amen.

GUARDIAN ANGEL PRAYER

Angel of God my Guardian dear, to whom God's love entrusts me here, ever this day be at my side to light and guard, to rule and guide. Amen.

PRAYER TO SAINT ALPHONSUS LIGUORI

Great servant of God and faithful conqueror of scrupulosity, pray that I too may bear this cross with patience and simplicity of heart, relying not on my own strength, but on the grace of God.

HELPFUL BOOKS

Here are some helpful books and booklets for the scrupulous. If you choose to read these (or any other) books, remember that it is not required to read the every page immediately. Instead, reading a little at a time, taking in one concept at a time, works best. When you come across a helpful idea, it is good to underline it or to write it down, so that it can be easily referenced in the future.

Pardon and Peace by Father Alfred Wilson, Roman Catholic Books.

This book contains many fascinating insights into the Sacrament of Reconciliation, often times with a great sense of humor from the author. Father Wilson points out some common, emotionally based, misconceptions that hinder our spiritual progress and he gives clear, simple advice on how to overcome them. This book is a treasure.

Achieving Peace of Heart by Fr. Narciso Irala, Roman Catholic Books.

Among other things, Fr. Irala provides simple solutions for effective decision-making and overcoming unreasonable fears. For example, the more vague a fear is, the more control it has over someone. Therefore, it is very beneficial to identify *exactly what one is afraid of*. This will enable him to see the problem clearly and take the necessary steps to overcome it.

Uniformity With God's Will by Saint Alphonsus Liguori, TAN Books.

Our great patron reminds us that God wills our good infinitely better than we could ever do it ourselves, so that nothing happens without God willing it—either directly or indirectly. Saint Alphonsus helps us to get out of our own mental prison and gain a better perspective on life, accepting all things peacefully as they come from the hand of God.

Prayer—Great Means of Grace, TAN Books.

Underscoring the necessity of prayer, this booklet is very helpful for those who want to think their way out of problems, without reference to God. Prayer is a much surer means to problem solving, as it unites us with our loving Father who knows what we need infinitely better than we do, and who has all the solutions to our problems. Saint Alphonsus says that he who prays is certainly saved.

BIBLIOGRAPHY

Hebert, Victoria and Bauer, Jody. *Wit and Wisdom of the Saints.* Liguori, MO: Liguori Publications, 2002.

Johnston, Francis. *Voice of the Saints.* Rockford, IL: TAN Books, 1987.

Jones, Frederick M. *Alphonsus de Liguori: Saint of Bourbon Naples.* Liguori Publications, 1992.

Kowalska, St. Faustina. *Divine Mercy in My Soul.* Stockbridge, MA: Marian Press, 2003.

Liguori, St. Alphonsus. *The Holy Eucharist.* Brooklyn: Redemptorist Fathers, 1934.

Liguori, St. Alphonsus. *The Great Means of Salvation and of Perfection.* Brooklyn: Redemptorist Fathers, 1927.

Liguori, St. Alphonsus. *The True Spouse of Jesus Christ (The Nun Sanctified).* Brooklyn: Redemptorist Fathers, 1929.

Liguori, St. Alphonsus. *Preparation for Death.* Brooklyn: Redemptorist Fathers, 1926.

Lisieux, St. Therese (of). *Story of a Soul.* Rockford, IL: TAN Books, 1997.

O'Hare, Msgr. Michael. *The Facts About Luther.* Rockford, IL: TAN Books, 1994.

Ruffin, Bernard C. *Padre Pio: the True Story, Revised and Expanded.* Huntington, IN. Our Sunday Visitor, 1991.

Trochu, Abbe Francis. *The Cure of Ars.* Rockford, IL. TAN Books, 1982.

The *Catechism of the Council of Trent* has been used in this work because it addresses concerns for the scrupulous more explicitly than the *Catechism of the Catholic Church.*

Under the heading of the Sacrament of Penance and Reconciliation (Nos. 1422-1498), the *Catechism of the Catholic Church* describes the principles and sacramental actions that provide individuals forgiveness for sin. The *Catechism of the Catholic Church* frequently refers to the canons and decrees of the Council of Trent and to the *Catechism of Trent* in this section.

The HAYDOCK

Douay-Rheims

Bible

Old and New Testaments
With Commentary

Filled with commentary, and including a dictionary of Biblical terms and names, this famous bible gets its name from the fact that in the 19th century the Rev. George Haydock collected commentary from many of the Fathers & Doctors and appended it to every page of the Douay. Many pages are at least 1/2 to 2/3 commentary on the text, hence the large format. This is the newest edition of what was the most common bible in all Catholic homes from the 1840's to well into the 20th century. The family history pages, Bible History section, and Bible Dictionary make it the most complete family Douay available today. It is eminently suitable for gift giving at weddings or other special occasions.

Gold leaf image on burgundy bonded leather cover
One Volume — Satin ribbon marker
 8 1/2" x 11" format — 1932 Pages — $125.00

www.loretopubs.org

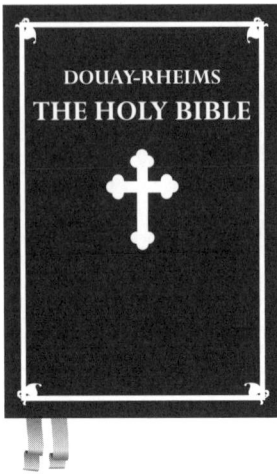

Handy Size Douay-Rheims Holy Bible

Bonded Leather Edition

Compared to the more modern editions of holy writ, the centuries old Douay is the most loyal of all to the literal meaning of the inspired text. If you wish to give someone the written word of God as a gift, why not fulfill that to the letter with this time honored edition. Wrapped in black bonded leather, it makes a perfect gift. This handy size bible (5.5" x 8.5") has a clear and readable typeface.

Bonded leather hardcover – 1,392 pages
Satin ribbon page markers – $39.95

The Purgatorian Manual

Containing Spiritual Readings and Prayers
This little handbook is only 3.75" x 5.75" and less than 3/4 inch thick, yet it contains over 300 pages. Printed with a beautiful full color cover, this book contains every prayer, meditation, novena, and Mass for the Holy souls that you could imagine. It is a treasure for those who love the Holy Souls and is priced to sell in quantity.

Price $8.00 —Special Discounts: 5-9 copies - $6.00 each, 10 or more $5.00 each

THE GREAT COMMENTARY ON THE GOSPELS

BY CORNELIUS ALAPIDE, S.J.

QUOTES FROM THE REVIEW by SCOTT HAHN

Cornelius aLapide, S.J. (1568-1637) is a giant figure in the history of Catholic biblical interpretation. Born in a tiny Catholic enclave in the Calvinist Netherlands in the bloody generation after the Reformation, aLapide grew to be one of the Church's most gifted scholars and spiritual interpreters of the sacred page.

Between 1614 and 1645, aLapide wrote commentaries on every book of Scripture except Job and Psalms.

To read aLapide four hundred years later is to enter a nearly forgotten world of biblical interpretation ...more striking – the sheer breadth and density of aLapide's interpretative matrix or his audacity in summoning all these resources to the interpretation of the sacred text.

aLapide himself takes a breathtakingly high view of Scripture's purpose... aLapide also prefaces his commentary with thirty-eight "canons of interpretation," which reflect a wise and prayerful method. " It is clear that the Fathers hold pride of place for aLapide in his interpretative work.

• **6"x 9" Book format • 2900+ Pages in four volumes • First complete English translation • Sewn Binding & Headbands • Bonded Leather Covers & Satin Ribbons • Greatest Catholic Bible Commentary ever • Extensive discussion of Greek and Hebrew words • $199. Complete set**

A List of Other Small Books
Available from Loreto Publications

Loreto Publications
P. O. Box 603
Fitzwilliam, NH 03447
Phone: 603-239-6671
www.LoretoPubs.org